Advance Praise

I love to read books that feel real and authentic from the get-go. While Megan states in the introduction that she was going to be vulnerable in writing this book, she writes in such a way that the reader forgets she said that and feels very drawn into her experiences, feelings, and life. I felt right there with her as the bottom fell out from under her. I felt as though I could have been the friend who said, "Put on your big girl panties and get back to living life." I felt that I was truly along for the ride.

The Selfish Hour is all about a journey to self-care, one that we each take, just in different ways. Megan has a wonderful way of telling her story that draws the reader right alongside. She is honest and vulnerable and real about her experiences. She's lived, learned and lived some more, all with the understanding that she is wonderfully made and has a gift to be shared through her authenticity. This is definitely a book I will read again, and share with clients, colleagues, and friends as we are each on a journey that includes learning from the experiences of others

— **Cathy Agasar**, detox and wellness specialist, health coach, and bestselling author of *The Gift of Loss*

Megan Weisheipl did a brilliant job of immediately drawing me into her beautiful story of self-discovery and carrying me through each step of her process of transformation. I could so easily relate to her thoughts and felt like I was right there with her through every selfish hour. Her vulnerability is so powerful and her dedication to becoming the best version of herself was raw and influential. You cannot read this book and not be inspired to improve your mindset, too, through your version of your own selfish hours.

— **Jackie Carl**, life coach for entrepreneurs

In *The Selfish Hour*, Megan Weisheipl inspires readers to embark on a transformative journey of self-discovery and liberation. With relatable stories and insights, Megan illustrates how dedicating a daily "selfish hour" can lead to powerful change. The poignant question most women ask themselves at some point, "How did I even get here?" is thoughtfully explored, as Megan shows how changing our old stories and thoughts about ourselves can create a brighter and more fulfilling life.

This book is a must-read for anyone seeking personal growth and transformation, and it offers a powerful reminder of the importance of self-reflection in shaping our lives. As Megan reminds us, the stories we tell ourselves ultimately become our reality.

— **Rachel K. Hudson,** certified life and
relationship coach

Megan Weisheipl's book, *The Selfish Hour*, is an engaging and entertaining self-help book that starts by taking us through her journey of corporate America and the lessons and hardships she learned along the way. From fancy cars, being at the top of her game, and being miserable on the inside resulted in an all-time low feeling torn. She questioned what had happened to her life. It prompted her wanting to and leaving the bureaucracy of big business to find true passion and balance in her life.

So relatable and refreshing to hear the real-life scenario between her ears, and she grits through. This book will take you through a gamut of emotions. I chuckled at her humor, teared up with her vulnerability as I felt like it paralleled my own, and felt inspired by this thought-provoking easy page-turner. This will be a raw and authentic book if you want to stop the pity party and get inspired to make things happen. I recommend it to anyone ready to shine a light on themselves, reflect on their journey, and unlock their true potential.

—**Jill Jensen**, CEO, Jill and Mike Get Active

Megan Weisheipl has simplified the art of taking your power back through this personal tale of self-discovery. Her words and relatable stories streamline the age-old problem of getting out of your own way. As modern women it's incredible how limiting our internal voices can be when we are forced to make life choices. In this book Megan explores ways to allow that internal voice to evolve into an empowering motivator by changing our own story. Her memories are so raw you can't help but feel her vulnerability and then relish in her rise as she realizes she is more than her past. Every woman can benefit from these inspirational words.

— **Ashley Kreutzer,** vice president, Ram-T Corporation

From my perspective as a health coach, I was expecting this book to reinforce the value of self-care for each individual, but this is so much more! Megan bared her soul as she takes us on her journey through success and devastation and shows us how to sort through the stories we play out in our heads and discover who we are ... and it's not what we thought. I have been on this journey myself and, while it could be easy to look at the many ups and downs in my life as negative, I really appreciate what Megan points out, "Look at your past as the foundation that set you up to be the person you are today. Say thank you for the lessons learned ... and then say goodbye to the limitations." This is the key to personal growth. Give yourself the gift, no matter your age, of embarking on the journey with Megan as your guide and your wings will be released for you to soar.

— **Kelly Lutman**, certified functional medicine health coach, Pursue Wellness for You, and author of *Thriving Through Cancer*

Megan has written a book for anyone who has asked themselves, "Is this all there is?" or "When does my real-life start?" Her relatable personal stories guide readers to explore their own stories, answer questions, and figure out their own happy ending.

— **Connie Jo Miller**, author of *Words of Whimsy*
trilogy and bookkeeper, Enigma Bookkeeping
Solutions

Women tend to find themselves attempting to balance multitudes of responsibilities associated with career and family. Unfortunately, constant juggling of tasks for others with no rest can result in feelings of burnout, emptiness, and lack of purpose. In addition, insufficient self-care can negatively impact health and wellness. *The Selfish Hour* is a powerful testimonial to the importance of digging deep to find happiness. Megan takes readers on a riveting journey of finding life satisfaction through self-reflection and giving herself permission to take the needed time to care for herself. What a beautiful message we can all learn from.

— **Gina Ramsey**, author of *Burnt Gloveboxes*

The Selfish Hour is exactly what everyone needs in this fast paced, noisy, get-it-all-done type of world we live in. The reminder to look deep within ourselves and be vulnerable is such a power message so many of us need to hear to become the best version of ourselves, find a deeper meaning, go after our audacious goals, and ultimately live the juiciest life imaginable.

— **Erika Rothenberger**, director of performance systems, Henkels & McCoy and TEDx speaker

Reflective, relatable, and relevant. Megan takes you on a journey that mirrors the experiences of so many women. There were tears, laughter, and inspiration—reading *The Selfish Hour* truly like felt chatting with a dear friend. If you're ready to become the new definition of "selfish," this book is for you!

—**Jessica Stewart**, personalized learning coach

The Selfish Hour

The Selfish Hour

Transform Your Life in One Hour a Day

Megan Weisheipl

Edited by
Deborah Kevin

HIGHLANDER
PRESS

THE SELFISH HOUR. Copyright © 2023 by Megan Weisheipl

ISBN: 978-1-956442-13-7
Ebook ISBN: 978-1-956442-14-4
Library of Congress Control Number: 2023934041

Published by Highlander Press
501 W. University Pkwy, Ste. B2
Baltimore, MD 21210

Editor: Deborah Kevin (deborahkevin.com)
Cover design: Hanne Broter (yourbrandvision.com)
Author photos: Heike Martin

To Nick, Codi, and Devney:
Thank you for loving me and giving me the space to grow into the woman I am today. You are my everything.

Contents

Introduction

> If you are powerful enough to create a negative story and believe it to the point that it controls the scope of your life, you are also powerful enough to change that narrative and create whatever life you desire.
>
> — Megan Weisheipl

I had an identity crisis.

At thirty-five years old, I got to figure out who I really was, and what I really wanted from life. This book is about that journey. About how I transformed my thoughts, my beliefs—and ultimately my whole life—in just one hour a day. Through these pages, I share how the stories I created in my childhood were the filters I ran all of my experiences through, and how these childhood stories unconsciously controlled everything I did.

Essentially this book is about how I learned to understand how my mind works, and the process I used to redirect my thought patterns in order to transform my life.

Before that, I felt like I was living two lives: the one that everybody saw, and the one that was happening in my mind. I didn't understand how there could be such a disconnect between the two, so I held it inside, until one day my husband asked me a simple question: "Why do you act like that?" and it changed my life forever.

The subsequent process of self-discovery was certainly not quick or easy, but it *was* highly addictive. I became a dedicated student of my own inner workings. I wanted to know why I thought the way I thought, and I wanted to one day share my journey with others, and help them to understand their own messed up minds. I wanted to teach people how to turn their confusion into something beautiful and useful.

One of the most important things I have learned thus far, is how powerful our thoughts really are. They are the epicenter of everything. They control how we feel, how we act, and ultimately how we choose to live our lives. Until we fully embrace the process of understanding our minds and unlearn some of our unconscious behaviors, we might never regain control of our lives.

We have unconsciously learned how to view the world through a pair of glasses we put on as kids. Unfortunately, these glasses are clouded with beliefs we inherited from our parents, clogged up with our cultural and environmental conditioning, and full with straight up stories we created in our youth that have played on repeat until they became imbedded beliefs that rule our lives.

A belief is nothing more than a thought that has been reinforced enough times for it to take the shape of rock-solid truth in our minds. *We* give the thought its power. Oftentimes, a belief is based on something someone said, did, or even didn't do that we assigned a meaning to. For every circumstance in our lives, we have a choice in the meaning we give to it. Two people can watch the exact same thing happen, but they may assign completely different meanings due to the unique filters they have in their minds.

Until I embarked on my journey toward self-understanding, the meaning I assigned to everyday situations was based purely on the beliefs I created from circumstances in my childhood. Every interaction, conversation, commercial on TV—everything—was run through this filter. I justified my beliefs by telling myself, *It's how I was raised,* or *It's just who I am,* but ultimately these were just excuses.

Let me elaborate. When I use the word *story,* what I mean is the thoughts we tell ourselves and others about a particular event. There is the fact (what actually happened) and then our interpretation of the fact. Our story is much more entertaining than the boring facts, so we tend to spice it up and repeat the new version to ourselves and to others, until (in our minds at least) this story becomes fact.

Oftentimes, the version of the story we tell ourselves has a negative context with a baseline *not enough* belief. You might be able to recognize and identify with some of these *not enough* statements:

- I'm not smart enough to work there.
- I'm not worthy enough to hang out in that crowd.
- I'm not lovable enough to be in a healthy relationship.
- I'm not good enough to really care about my health and appearance.
- I'm just not enough.

In the coming pages, I share my own stories and explain how they affected my life. I also share how I learned to change my relationship to these stories and use their power for good, instead of for self-sabotage, victimization, and pity parties as I used to. I learned how to identify my past beliefs, how to separate them from the facts, and how to build a relationship with my past that allowed it to propel me forward instead of holding me back. If you manage to learn only one thing from this book, let it be this:

 If you are powerful enough to create a negative story and believe it to the point that it controls the scope of your life, you are also

powerful enough to change the narrative and create whatever life you desire.

The direction your life takes is completely under your control, and it all starts with your thoughts. If you have ever thought, *If I could just get out of my own way*, or *Why does it seem to work out so easily for everyone else but not me?* well my friend, buckle up your seat belt because you are in for a ride. Enjoy this journey to YOU!

Part One

Caught Up in the Noise

> *Sometimes I wonder if all of this is happening because I didn't forward that email to 15 people.*
>
> — Anonymous

It was still dark outside, but my mind was wide awake. I rolled over to look at the clock and, just as I figured, it was 5:12 a.m. My body naturally wakes up between 5 and 5:20 a.m. each day, and I still have a slight sense of pride when I wake up before my alarm, because I find it fascinating that my mind knows when to wake up. It only took a few days to train myself to wake up at this time, and that was one of the actions that started the shift in my life.

- Do I always want to get out of my comfy bed? *No.*
- Do I always want to stumble to the bathroom in the dark and then upstairs to my office? *No.*
- Do I tiptoe as quietly as possible so as not to wake anyone? *Yes!*

My Selfish Hour happens between 5:30 and 6:30 a.m., and I won't allow anyone to disrupt it. It has become sacred to me. It was during this time that I rediscovered myself. During one hour each morning for two years, I transformed my thoughts, my feelings, my actions, and ultimately my life when I retrained the thought patterns in my mind.

In this book, I share that journey with you and teach you how to do the same if you choose to.

I'm guessing since you are holding this book, that you are ready to retrain your mindset. My intention in sharing some of the more intimate details of my life is not for you to get to know me better, which will happen by default anyway, but the reason I allow myself to be so vulnerable is so that you can use this book as a mirror to look deep within and be vulnerable with yourself too.

I share the darkness and ugliness I hid from for most of my life, and while I may be uncomfortable with people learning about the skeletons in my closet, it is worth it. I share myself with you as someone who has been in your shoes, who has had (and still has) crazy thoughts, and who has felt those extreme highs and lowest of lows. I want you to know that you too can change, and that there is hope for you to live an amazing life; a life you may have deemed perfect for others but not for you. It can be yours too if you want it.

I share all the realizations, and the "ah-ha" moments I had during those early morning hours in the hope that you will have "ah-ha" moments of your own. I encourage you to keep a journal as you read this book. Write down the thoughts that come to you. You may even have a thought surface that you haven't had in years; it's coming up for a reason, so give it attention and figure out why. Maybe even read this book with a tissue handy; I am known for making my clients and students cry sometimes too. I used to apologize for it and feel really bad for making people cry, but I have learned that it means I have done my job in creating a safe space for you to feel the feelings you may have closed off a long time ago.

Crying is not a weakness. It means there is hidden pain that yearns to be healed. Stop pushing the pain down. You no longer need to create a false sense of toughness. It's time to deal with buried pain, learn from it, heal, and become a better person because of it. The struggles you face are all a test, and as you overcome these obstacles your confidence will grow, and your testimony will be created. Too many people use their difficulties as a stop sign, and then live a life of suffering while wondering why they can't get ahead. We look to our past for evidence of what we're capable of in the future, and in doing so we dramatically limit ourselves. Our past lives in our thoughts and has no control over our future...unless we allow it to.

One of the keys to moving forward in a purposeful way and creating the future you want, is learning how to reframe your past and using that knowledge to empower you. You cannot change your past no matter how ugly, terrible, or traumatic it may have been, but it is important to acknowledge it, learn the lesson, and grow from it. Just make sure you don't define yourself by it. Look at your past as the foundation that set you up to be the person you are today. Say thank you for the lessons learned and how they shaped you, and then say goodbye to the limitations.

Growing through this process won't be easy. You will have to face things about yourself that you have buried so deep inside that you completely forgot they even happened. If you just had the thought, *I don't want to go there*, that is the Universe giving you a friendly tap on the shoulder and nudging that it is in fact time. It is no coincidence you are holding this book. You are ready.

Dive into this book with the intention of creating awareness and enabling change. You may learn things about yourself that provide you with clarity on why you think, feel, and act the way you do in certain situations, in your relationships, and in all of your everyday life circumstances. Maybe you never even realized how your past has affected your life, but I will help you change the lens through which you view yourself and the world around you.

DURING THE PANDEMIC, I COULD EASILY HAVE MADE THE excuse not to wake up early because I really had no reason to do so, but I refused to let the pandemic wreck my schedule. Whether it was cold and dark, or the sun was brightly shining, I followed my routine because doing so made me whole. If I didn't stick to my routine, my mind would likely have gone to an extremely dark and oddly comfortable place.

During the early days of the pandemic I had a moment. Okay, I had several moments. Okay, it turned into six hours of worry, but no one would have guessed because that whole time I hid behind a smile on my face.

After my morning meditation, my thumb hit the Facebook button on my phone, and from there I quickly spiraled into doom and gloom. My mind instantly sunk into fear and scarcity, and I operated from that space. Instead of spending my time working on myself, or reading a book that inspired me, I went downstairs, put on my coat and shoes, and snuck out of the house. I can definitely say that this was a particularly odd challenge for me because I am not one to leave the house without "putting my face on" as my mom used to call it. I hadn't brushed my teeth, washed my face, put on a bra, or even changed out of my pajamas. I was basically a walking Walmart meme, but I didn't care.

I was consumed by worry and fear over what being on "lockdown" even meant, but I dressed it up as "taking care of my family" as I made my eighth grocery shopping trip in five days. Ninety dollars later, I unloaded groceries and stocked basement shelves (because our upstairs pantry was already full), and I felt my old friend anxiety giving me a hug again.

My family weren't aware that I had gone shopping before they awoke, so I put on my happy mom and wife face, cooked breakfast, and while they ate, I slipped away to finally clean myself up and get dressed for the day. I worked for a few hours with an underlying panic growing in me. *How will our economy survive? How will we survive? How long will this last? What will the new normal be? Will this be the next Great Depression? Will my husband lose his job?*

With these questions pinging through my mind, my anxiety feasted on them like it had been in hibernation. I couldn't focus, my fingers kept clicking on articles I shouldn't be reading because each article was flooded with bad news and my fear was growing. I was caught in a negative cycle but couldn't stop, like a car accident that you can't look away from. A few hours later, I sat cross-legged on our bed while my husband Nick folded clothes. I asked, "Are you scared?"

I felt instantly annoyed with his nonchalant response, "Of what?" I felt like he should know exactly what had been going on in my mind for the previous six hours.

I cleared my throat and rephrased my question. "With our economy, our world, and everything that is happening right now. Are you scared?"

He didn't stop his folding rhythm, and in true Nick-fashion replied, "Nope, it's outside my control. The only thing we can control is staying home and hunkering down."

After ten years of marriage, I had grown accustomed to his emotionless, matter-of-fact answers. Letting out a big sigh backed with fear I said, "This is the first day I am scared. I'm scared we are going into a recession."

There are so many reasons Nick is the person God created for me, but his response in that moment topped the list. "What do you know about economics?"

I gave him the blank stare and smirked. "Nothing. I hated that fucking class in college." With that statement, I unconsciously gave myself permission to release all my anxiety, and for the worry to leave my body. I had been so focused on what I couldn't control, I forgot to focus on the one thing I have worked so hard to control: my thoughts. That quick conversation helped me to realize I was operating from a place of scarcity, which was why I felt like we did not have enough food or supplies, even though we could have survived for two months without leaving the house.

My life was about thought work, abundance, love, and sharing my knowledge with others. I taught my students to focus on what they could control, which was their thoughts. However, that morning I had forgotten everything I knew and gotten caught up in the noise.

The reason I share this story to open my book is simple: even though I eat, sleep, and breathe what I teach, I experience the human process just like everyone else. I can get caught up in old thought patterns, and in the noise, and operate from a place of fear. Each of us is a work in progress, trying daily to be the best versions of ourselves. Life has its own way of throwing challenges at us to see how we respond. A global pandemic with the economy basically shut down for who knew how long... well, that was a true test of staying positive, finding a silver lining, and living all the cliches you could conjure.

A silver lining of the pandemic for me was that I had been trying to write this book for a while. My biggest hurdle was a story I told myself: I was not a writer. I read books, but I didn't write them. I was a speaker, and shifting my mindset to writing posed a challenge for me. My drive to help was bigger than my excuse that I was not a writer, and I reminded myself of my bigger mission several times a day, sometimes several times an hour.

I know this book will change the lives of the people who allow themselves to embrace it and go there. "Going there" means opening yourself up to see the real you that was buried under what other people think, cultural conditioning, and environmental factors. Allow yourself to go "there" in the pages to come. Do the work, be with yourself, and become a watcher of your thoughts. Journal. Do whatever it takes to go "there," because if you do, you will meet the wonderful, amazing, beautiful person who is inside of you: your authentic self.

Common Oxymoron

> There is no heavier burden than unfulfilled potential.
>
> — Charles M. Shultz

WHEN I WAS THIRTY-FIVE YEARS OLD, MY LIFE LOOKED PERFECT on the outside.

- I was married to a wonderful man named Nick.
- We had two beautiful daughters.
- I flourished in a successful career.
- We lived in a nice house.
- We had a great circle of friends.

I had achieved what I thought I always wanted, and yet I felt so conflicted every day because I still felt empty inside. I loved my husband, and I loved our girls. I loved our home. I was good at my job, and it paid me well. So, what the hell was wrong with me? Was I greedy? I thought I was ungrateful for what I had and was so ashamed by those feelings that I kept my emptiness a secret. I thought, *Stop wanting more. Stop taking for granted what others wish they had.* But the painted-on smile and fake laughter couldn't fill the hollowness inside my chest. I saw myself as a common oxymoron, successful yet unfulfilled.

One evening on a particularly tough day, a conversation that turned into an argument just happened to be one of the most pivotal moments of my life. A six-word sentence ending with a question mark changed the course of my life forever. When I reflect back, I realize that God had been trying to speak to me in several different ways, but I was too closed off to hear the message, so He used Nick.

Before I share that pivotal moment with you, let me tell you a little about me and my career, because for most of my twenties and part of my thirties that was the center of my life. Well, career and vodka if I'm being honest. I lived in Philadelphia, and I climbed the corporate ladder and made all the sacrifices one was supposed to make to win in the business world.

At twenty-five years old, I got hired for a position that evolved into one of the biggest blessings and biggest heartbreaks all rolled into one. I stayed at that industry for thirteen years. In 2005, I was hired as a mortgage loan officer. That job taught me one of the greatest life skills: how to communicate with people. Not simply how to talk to people, but how to really listen to what someone said, ask the right questions at the right times, and direct the conversation.

My job was to talk on the phone a minimum of three hours a day or make at least eighty dials. Everything was tracked. Each morning, the numbers from the previous day were posted for the whole office to see, and you were quickly judged by how effective your presence had been the day before.

I spent so much time in the office that the people there became my family. This was no nine-to-five job. There were times I was in the office at 7 a.m. on a Saturday or walking out to my car at 11 p.m. on a Tuesday. A normal day consisted of eating all three meals at the office, or having dinner and drinks at the bar with my co-workers, while discussing interest rates and loan-to-value ratios. I loved that job. It gave me purpose, and I felt I was building my career. I began making more money than both my parents put together, and that made me feel accomplished.

The next year, I drove a sports car and felt unstoppable. I did everything I was supposed to do: came in early, stayed late, and went above and beyond. My hard work and long hours paid off. I made it to the first rung of the corporate ladder and was promoted. As my career and paycheck grew, so did the emptiness I felt. I was caught in an achievement trap and kept striving for the next big accomplishment so that I would *feel* differently.

I remember telling a friend that when I looked at the trajectory of my life, I could see myself waking up one day to realize I had all the material things I could ever want, with awards hanging on the wall, but no one to share it with because I forgot to date. I felt I was a shell of a person walking around in designer suits with sassy high heels, driving a fast car, while my chest was as hollow as the Tin Man's from *The Wizard of Oz*.

Fast forward to 2007 when I was twenty-seven years old, and my sad plan came to fruition. I had not been on a date for more than a year because my work consumed me, promotions required more of my time and energy, and I falsely believed that through my work I was changing lives. Then something happened in May that put things in motion to recalibrate my life: The Mortgage Meltdown.

Each day I came into work and scanned the internet for something positive about our economy, but the only words I saw were bankrupt, foreclosure, and closing associated with companies just like mine. The economy was like a bucking bronco, no matter how strong your grip was on the rein you were bound to get thrown off. The industry was so fucked I believed it was only a matter of time before I was out of a job as well.

Everything we worked so hard to build in the preceding four years was disappearing, and there wasn't a damn thing we could do to save it. In an office with over 200 employees, we were down to ten in a matter of a couple of months. The fear, panic, and anxiety was palpable, but we made jokes and tried our best to stay positive while chewing on Pepto tablets to calm our nerves. Ten of us showed up every day with the determination to keep the doors open, but the storm proved to be much stronger than us.

December 7, 2007, the company I gave everything for was added to the mortgage implosion list and I lost my job. It was one of the saddest days of my life. It felt like a close friend had died. The people I considered family, with whom I loved spending my time, suddenly disappeared from my life. Many I have never seen in person again.

Not only did I lose my job and my work family, but I lost my home too. I was in the process of building a condo in downtown Philly. I'd picked out oak cabinets, granite countertops, and crown molding. I had put down a twenty-thousand-dollar deposit and given notice to my landlord. Within six months I went from living the high life to having nowhere to live, forfeiting my condo deposit to get out of the contract, selling my sports car, and moving in with my parents in Ohio. I joked that I moved out when I was eighteen and I knew everything, and moved back in at twenty-eight when I realized I knew nothing and was failing at life.

As I sat in my pink childhood bedroom, my dominant thought was, *What the fuck just happened to my life?* The change happened so fast my mind couldn't process it. I went for an entire week without speaking. I couldn't; there were no words to describe what had happened. I went numb. My mind spun over the speed and breadth of change without feeling like I had any control over it.

I drove around for hours reflecting on my past life in the city, a life seemingly full of opportunities and promise. Having lost everything, I found myself right back where I started. My sister-in-law tried to intervene, because she found me sleeping all day and going to the bar all night with the intention of living up to the country songs I heard on the radio. I was a good guitar riff of a sad story of love, loss, and looking for answers at the bottom of a bottle.

One morning, I decided it was time to visit a doctor to see if I was a good fit for anti-depressants. I thought maybe getting some "help" in the form of a daily pill would get me back on track to my happy self. I needed to stop the cycle of waking up, feeling like shit, and trying to sleep again hoping it would be different when I woke up the next time. But it never was. I couldn't live like that anymore. All the dreams I once had were gone, and I didn't even know where to look to find them again. I felt like I had had my shot at life and I blew it.

I showed up at the doctor's office feeling like I had admitted defeat with an attitude of "I can't do life; I'm not good at it. Can you give me some happy pills and I will be on my way?" When the doctor walked into the small and sterile room in an unfriendly manner, he asked me some very direct, yet broad questions.

Were you ever happy? "Well yes of course, but I lost my job, my house, and my life, and now I'm living back at my parents' house at twenty-eight years old while all my friends are getting married and moving on to the next stage."

When you get depressed what do you do? "I sleep and drink, and then I drink and sleep, hoping the next day will be better."

Have you ever spent a lot of money at one time? "Sure, I made 6-figures, my rent was $700 a month and I had a $300 car payment. I have spent over $1000 at the *Chanel* makeup counter because I could."

Do you ever feel you have had really high highs and really low lows? "Um, yeah... didn't you hear about *Chanel* makeup and now being in Brookfield, Ohio in a small doctors' office asking for antidepressants? I consider that pretty low."

Nine minutes later he said, "Sounds like you are bi-polar. I'm going to prescribe you some pills. Take them for thirty days and let me know how you feel."

I took the prescription, left his office, and drove back to my parents' house dumbfounded. I sat at the kitchen table and told my parents that a person I had never met before had asked me a few questions and in less than ten minutes had told me I was bi-polar, and that I should take different pills than I had gone there for. My innocent parent had heard of bi-polar, but only on TV or in the newspaper. They didn't know what to say other than, "Well, if that's what the doctor says, then you better take the pills."

I needed to not be around my parents at that moment, so I went to visit my cousin at her house down the street and told her my new life diagnosis. Her response was more like what I needed to hear: "What the fuck? You aren't bi-polar. You are simply lost in your life right now! I know you, and you don't need those pills. Snap out of it and get your shit straight." She speaks my language.

I left her house and called my best friend to tell her the news. Her response was completely different from the others: "I'm sorry to hear it, but it explains a lot. Now you have some answers and can start to get better."

The four people closest to me all had different perspectives on this new proposed life direction, but the only person who knows what's right for you is you. The nine minutes spent with the doctor that day did actually change the direction of life. I never filled the prescription, and I never went back to see that doctor, but he did give me the wakeup call to start dreaming again. I would like to think that that was his strategy all along—to scare me into thinking there was something bigger going on so I would snap out of it. Sadly, I don't think that was the case, but God played a bigger role in it for me than that doctor anyway.

Waterproof Mascara

> Every woman deserves a man to ruin her lipstick, not her mascara.

> — Charlotte Tilbury

AFTER A YEAR OF BOUNCING AROUND WITH NO DIRECTION FROM one odd job to the next, I found my way back to the mortgage business, which was like going back to an ex-boyfriend thinking maybe you had both changed during your time apart and things would be better this time. It started out all fun and exciting, but once I was deeply committed I realized the things that used to annoy me about him were still there, and he had also picked up some new annoying habits along the way.

Over the next couple of years, I worked my way back up the ladder, and Nick and I got married, started a family, and moved back to Philly for both of our careers. By 2015, I was the modern-day picture of a working mom. I woke up each morning around 6:30 a.m. to my youngest crying and babbling from her room. Then I would roll into our morning routine, which consisted of waking up our three-year-old, making breakfast, cleaning up, packing lunches, showering, getting everyone dressed, brushing teeth, giving hugs, saying, "I love you, have a great day," and heading out the door for daycare drop off and work.

My drive to work felt robotic: stuck in a line of cars driving in the same direction, parking in the same spot, and walking into the building at the same time, lunch bag in hand, ready to put in between eight and ten hours a day. I had been promoted to branch manager of a mortgage company about a year and half before and I had a love-hate relationship with my job. I loved that I was good at it, and it was an industry that gave me friendships, knowledge, sales education, and healthy paychecks, but I also held on to deep-seated bitterness from being burned years before.

As I rose up the corporate ladder, which is exactly what you think you want when you first start out: the title, the office, the responsibility; but all I became instead was a glorified babysitter and fire putter-outer. I had meetings about meetings, before meetings and after meetings. To get actual work done, I needed to come in early, stay late, or work weekends. Corporate America owned me. I spent ten years of my life working my tail off to be the first person to drop my kids off at daycare and the last to pick them up. I can vividly remember a time when my oldest daughter, Codi was about two years-old. I picked her up from daycare at six in the evening and brought her back to the office because Mama still had work to do. Thankfully, I had dual screens, so I put one screen on *Dora the Explorer* and worked on the other.

On our drive home, she said in her sweet Minnie Mouse-sounding voice, "Mommy, my belly hurts."

I realized at that moment that I hadn't fed her dinner. I was so focused on my work, that I had forgotten about my biggest responsi-bility in life. *What a horrible mother I am*, I thought as tears rolled down my cheeks. Of course, I didn't want to tell Nick, because I didn't want him thinking I totally suck as a wife and mother because there was no dinner on the table, it was time for bed, and our daughter was starving.

My internal conflict amplified as I was the breadwinner in our household, so being a mother and wife took a backseat to my career, which was the exact opposite of what I wanted but I was in so deep that I couldn't see a way out.

Then it happened: the phone call that changed everything. It was a Thursday in early September, and I heard the phone ringing from my office. I left the sales floor and ran to check the caller ID. Just as I figured, it was my boss and the call I was expecting. With a smile on my face, I shut the door and answered the phone with a cheerful, "Hey there!" I knew this was the phone call that was going to make all my sacrifices worthwhile. I had just finished my best month ever as a sales manager, and our office was number one in the company. I followed the numbers closely, because I was the youngest, and one of only two female branch managers in the whole company, so I felt an overwhelming need to prove myself. Needless to say, emotions were running high.

But this phone call was it, this was the congratulatory call that was going to make it all worth it—the years I put in before the mortgage meltdown, the year and half searching for answers in a bottle, and then the next five years climbing the corporate ladder rung by rung. I was about to have my name associated with the top dogs of the company. I was putting my female stamp in the top managers club. And I was ready.

The conversation began, and the longer he talked, the faster my red lipstick smile disappeared. Instead of saying, "Great job last month, your office performed at such a high level and we appreciate you working so hard," he talked about, "Restructuring the office and it would only be a temporary hit to my income, but if I put my focus on hiring more people, I would build it back up over the next year."

I paced around my office because I could not believe the noise on the other end of the line.

Then he said it, a sentence that is tattooed in my mind forever:

"The owner of the company said if I don't cut your paycheck, he is cutting mine."

The response in my head was, *Are you fucking kidding me?* I don't remember exactly what I actually said, but I had too much couth to drop the f-bomb I wanted to. The bottom line was the owner of the company thought I was making too much money, and he gave an ultimatum to my boss: his paycheck or mine... someone needed to make less money.

Ten years of hard work, dedication, and sacrificing family time led to that moment when I realized I was only a number. I didn't matter to the company; I was just a person holding a spot, and I felt trapped. I needed that job and the income. Nick was looking for a new job, we had a baby and a toddler in daycare, and my shoulders bent with the weight of it all. Corporate America was strangling me, and I had never felt smaller in all my life.

I hung up the phone, slumped down in my big office chair, put my head on the desk, and cried. My work felt meaningless. *I* felt meaningless. I'm even struggling to type this, because reliving the moment weighs me down. The worst part was, that on the other side of my door, an office full of people were so excited because they knew we were the number one office in the company. They felt proud and had worked hard to keep the momentum going, and I as their leader was responsible for keeping the energy high.

I thanked God for waterproof mascara, because it helped me to mask what I felt inside. I got out my purse mirror, wiped the tears from my eyes, put on the all too familiar fake smile, pressed my internal button to turn on the cheerful personality, opened the office door, and continued on with my day like nothing happened. I should have won an Oscar for that performance.

That evening, I uncharacteristically left the office on time. As I got into my car, I saw the bottle of celebratory *Prosecco* I had picked up on my lunch break in the passenger seat. That gesture sent me into a tailspin of ugly crying and swearing. *How am I supposed to tell Nick?* He was unemployed and dealing with his own issues of self-worth and life direction. My role in our relationship at that time was the rock, but at that moment I felt more like liquid goo.

Nick and I are two of the most dedicated, hardworking, and loyal people you will ever meet, so how was it that one of us was unemployed and the other felt meaningless in her career? Sometimes in life you stop, look around, and wonder, "How did I even get here?"

That was the beginning of the end of my time in the mortgage industry.

The Question "Why?"

I PARKED THE CAR IN OUR DRIVEWAY AND SAT THERE FOR WHAT felt like an eternity allowing my waterproof mascara to do its job before I got out of the car. The bottle of *Prosecco* transformed into a "drink your sorrows away" bottle, so I grabbed it and headed into the house.

Nick was in the kitchen getting dinner ready. He was in between coaching jobs and had been for the previous year. He fell in love with baseball when he was two years-old, and the love affair never stopped. He played through high school and college, and he played professionally in Germany before becoming a coach after his playing career came to an end from a partially-torn rotator cuff. A month before our daughter Codi was born, we moved to Philadelphia when he got a Division 1 pitching coach job. He quit that job after two seasons. Nick is extremely intelligent, strategic with every move, and has a passion deeper than anyone I have ever met. The job we moved states for, ultimately didn't align with his values.

When Nick quit that job, I watched him change. He didn't know how to be without baseball in his life. Recruiting, coaching, strategizing, the clink of the ball hitting the bat, and throwing batting practice; baseball was his first true love. When it was no longer a part of his life, the joy left his eyes. He didn't say as much, he didn't laugh as much, and he slept on the couch. I knew it wasn't about me, but the love of his life was missing, and I took the hit for it. For richer or poorer, good times or bad, in sickness and health; I'd made these vows, and I took pride in being the steady partner during this time. However, after a year and half of being the financial and emotional rock, I was exhausted to breaking point.

It hit me on that day: I was done. I was empty. I had nothing more to give anyone. I set the sad bottle of Prosecco on the countertop and plopped down at the kitchen table. Nick could tell something was wrong, so he asked me to tell him what happened, but my explanation somehow escalated into an argument. My emotions were high, low, and all over the place, and he was the person taking the emotional punches from my day.

We started arguing and, like a script I had memorized, I said the same words I often said when we had a difference of opinion. The script sounded like this: "You're right. I'm wrong. You're superior, I'm inferior." Let this be very clear: Nick did nothing to ignite this response from me. It was just my "go-to" in this type of situation.

My entire body language changed during those interactions, with my shoulders slumped over, my voice soft like a shy kid, and my energy diminished.

But, on this particular day, Nick didn't keep trying to win his point, he simply said, "Why do you do that, why do you act that way?"

I wanted to scream back, "YOU make me act this way!" but that day I heard the question differently. I stopped, let out a sigh, and thought, "Why *do* I act this way?"

The question repeated over and over again in my mind, but I had no answer. Nick continued, "You are a successful, professional woman in charge of millions of dollars, and an office of people, but then you act like this; I just don't get you."

He has a unique ability to take the emotion out of things. I am not gifted with said ability, I go from zero to a hundred with full emotion. He was totally right, and, dammit, I hated when he was right, especially when I was supposed to be the strong one in our life then. The fight quickly dissipated because my mind went to another world. I no longer cared about what had happened that day. My job and my external world were a reflection of my internal struggle. Why was I insecure on the inside but exuded what others perceived as confidence on the outside?

The phone call from my boss and Nick's "why" were responsible for the rerouting of my life. The lens through which I viewed the world, myself, and basically everything, changed that day. The new lens caused me not only to look at things differently, but to question everything. And I mean everything.

That night as I lay in bed, my mind spun with so many questions, and none of them had to do with work. Work was the least of my concerns. I knew I wasn't valued at the company, and that knowledge made me take a deeper look. I realized I didn't value myself and needed to start there first.

That sleepless night, I had an epiphany: "My life is reactionary. I operate with no intentionality. I just go through the motions each day." Each morning, I woke up to my children and instantly went into mom mode, and from there to work mode, and then back to mom and wife mode. I was so exhausted I usually fell asleep on the couch with a half drank glass of wine while watching TV with Nick.

Was my life even my own? I felt I was in my own *Groundhog Day* movie, except there was no Bill Murray, and no groundhog; just me as mom, boss, wife, rinse, and repeat. My life had become about everyone else; it had nothing to do with me. I was just a shell of a person going through the motions and doing it rather well... or so I thought. I worked hard as a mommy, wife, and boss to fill everyone's cup and make sure all were taken care of, but I didn't even know where my cup was and for so long had never even thought about it. It was probably spilled in the living room, leaving a stain behind the couch that I would eventually find and clean up. I started to think I wasn't just in *Groundhog Day*, but I was also Michael J. Fox in *Back to the Future* where he held the picture of his family and people faded out of it. That was me. I was fading out of our family picture and no one knew it but me. This middle of the night epiphany shed a light on why I had been feeling so empty inside.

The next day, as I grabbed the regular foods I always picked up and tossed in my cart, I stopped in my tracks. A deafening stream of questions spun through my mind. I was in such a habit of buying, cooking, and eating the same foods, I began to wonder if I even liked what I was buying; or did I grab the same stuff because that was just what I did?

I had a mini breakdown in the grocery store and walked around for forty-five minutes looking up and down aisles without putting anything in my cart. Again, thank God for waterproof mascara to stop the flow of black tears making streams down my face. I walked out of the store having bought only a few random things, got into my car, and hit my head on the steering wheel. *What the hell was going on with me? I couldn't even grocery shop.* I felt heavy. I felt lost. I felt like an imposter living a life I created but didn't know how to function in anymore. But, of course, I wouldn't ask for help or tell anyone, because I had too much pride for that.

The questions swarmed in my mind. I felt like a cartoon character with the word bubble above me, the words moving so fast anyone would be exhausted reading them:

- Do I have a true relationship with my friends, or do we just hang out because we live near each other?
- If the mortgage career isn't for me, what am I supposed to do?
- What is my purpose?
- Why do I want to travel the world?
- What do I really enjoy doing?

- Do I even like Taco Tuesday, or do I do it because that is what we do every Tuesday?
- And the billion-dollar question...who am I?

The can was opened and worms were everywhere!

The Selfish Hour

> Until you value yourself, you will not value your time.
> Until you value your time, you will not do anything
> with it.
>
> — M. Scott Peck

I FELT A STRONG CALLING TO FIND ANSWERS TO ALL OF THOSE
questions, and an even stronger inclination to understand and release
the insecurities I had unknowingly been living with all of my life. It
was time to truly get to know myself and understand what the hell
caused me to feel empty.

Since I had designed my life to be about everyone and everything
except me, I got to do something different, and the only time I had
was early in the morning before my family woke up. I am not a night
owl and my mind is mush after 7 p.m., so in the morning it had to be.

I set my alarm for 5:30 a.m. and went to bed, ready to wake up
earlier and start a new routine. I made a non-negotiable agreement
with myself that I'd avoid social media and emails during that hour. It
was an hour for me to be selfish and only focus on figuring me out.

Most people, especially moms, view being selfish as a negative. No one wants to identify with being selfish because that would make them a bad person. I came up with my own definition of selfish, so please adopt it if you want. Selfish means:

Taking care of oneself first, and filling your cup so you can pour more into others'. Being selfish means you care so much about others that you put yourself first to be your best for yourself and everyone else. Selfish means love for oneself first.

My alarm went off at 5:30 a.m., and I jumped out of bed and went upstairs to my office, but I had zero game plan of what I would do to fill an hour. I had been intrigued by the idea of meditating and knew lots of people who did it, so I thought that might be a good place to start. I turned on my computer, pulled up YouTube.com and typed in the search bar "meditation for beginners," then clicked on a ten-minute meditation, popped in my air pods, and closed my eyes.

I was not good at sitting still, and my monkey mind threw to-do lists at me and reminded me of everything I forgot to do the day before. I believed that meditation made you shut your mind off, and all the answers to all the questions just flooded in. Yes, that can happen, but...meditation is a learned practice that takes time. Obviously, my patience was not at its best. Instead, in those ten minutes my mind wandered to work, what I needed to do, the kids, house stuff, bills—everything but the answers I sought.

Meditation ate up ten minutes, but what was I supposed to do with the remaining fifty? I did what any smart, educated, and lost woman would do: I googled "Oprah."

Oprah was my North Star, and I figured if anyone could help me it would be her, or at least she would point me in the right direction. I watched all kinds of Oprah videos and interviews while also checking out her hair styles through the years. She said things that made me think differently about myself, and afterwards I felt energized and motivated to start my day. After that first Selfish Hour, I was hooked. I wanted more "me time." For so many years, I thought me time meant getting my nails done, or going to the grocery store alone, but once I truly got a taste of some selfish time and my mind had been expanded, it couldn't go back to its original dimensions. I had so many questions, and I knew in my heart that the answers were held in that hour.

Each morning my alarm went off at 5:30 a.m., and I jumped out of bed and went to my office to meditate, and then I searched for Oprah's wisdom. I soaked it all in and spent countless mornings hanging out with her and taking notes. I watched when she spoke at university graduation ceremonies, and when she interviewed people I admired like Tony Robbins, and Dr. Wayne Dyer. I studied her when the roles were reversed, and she was the one being interviewed and replying to difficult questions. I binge watched her like a Netflix series. Journaling became a way for me to get my thoughts out and onto paper. Then I started a gratitude journal (because Oprah said I needed one) and bought books that she recommended. I was on a journey to reconnect to me, to the person I was before external influences affected my internal thoughts.

Nick began to notice a change in me, too. The words I spoke were more positive, I wasn't as stressed, and I began to dream again. The energy shifted in our house, and without me asking he got up with the girls, got them ready, packed lunches, and even made me a smoothie which he delivered to my office so I could have more time to myself. I began to think, *I'm really onto to something here.* Daily, for two straight years, from 5:30 a.m. to 6:30 a.m., I kept up my Selfish Hour, and it was truly one of the single best things I have ever done for myself.

During that time I got to know the one person I lived my entire life with but never really understood: me.

I am Stupid

> I felt I was beginning to figure out the secret to life: get up early, sit in silence, and connect with your soul.

— Megan Weisheipl

AROUND THE THIRD WEEK OF MY SELFISH HOUR, I NO LONGER needed the alarm to wake up. My mind and body knew, so I popped out of bed and quietly snuck upstairs. I fell in love with the stillness and silence of the early morning. **I felt I was beginning to figure out the secret to life: get up early, sit in silence, and connect with your soul.**

During those early morning hours, I started having flashbacks to my childhood. I quickly realized the only way to figure out my future was to go through my past. Old feelings that I thought I had done a great job of burying, or that I thought no longer mattered kept resurfacing.

Honestly, I secretly wished Oprah would just tell me what I was supposed to do, how to be exactly what God intended for me, and then I could go out and execute—so damn well! Unfortunately, that was not how it worked. I needed to figure it out on my own. Reliving old memories was uncomfortable. I didn't like experiencing things the first time around, so why would I want to open old wounds and experience them again in my mind a second or third time? No thank you!

An unknown energy kept pulling me toward working through whatever it was. I knew I would be better after tackling these memories head on, so I donned an invisible suit of armor and battled the demons from my past. I quickly realized that the thoughts and feelings I believed I had done a great job of burying deep inside, were the exact things that were running my life and had brought me to this breaking point. This just fueled my frustration because I thought I was past all of that junk, and yet there we were. I guess running from feelings, acting like they didn't matter, and drinking some spirits to drown them out wasn't the right way for me to live. I debunked my past, and it was troublesome.

From the videos I watched and the books I read, one theme stood out to me that I struggled with: the concept of "you create your own reality." I examined this from so many angles and just couldn't wrap my head around it. I had resistance to this idea, because I could come up with a long list of *"I didn't want to do that,"* and *"I didn't want to feel that way"* attached to experiences. I was too stubborn to accept the fact that I created the reality of any negative experiences, while at the same time being so ready for a change that I had only one choice and that was to surrender.

I surrendered the need to be right. I surrendered to the fact that I did not know all the answers, and I became open to learning. Hands down on this whole journey, the best thing I did was surrender and let go of control. Releasing the control noose of my own creation was incredibly liberating.

In one of the numerous Oprah videos I consumed, I learned that the beliefs we have today were created in our childhood. When I thought about my childhood, I couldn't think of anything bad that would have shaped my life. My parents weren't divorced. There were no major tragedies or deaths. Oh, how naive I was in thinking I was the exception to the rule!

All of my memories were good. Or—to be more specific—the memories I chose to remember were good. I grew up in a small country town in northeast Ohio, in a meticulously clean split style ranch house my parents had built on my grandfather's land next to the farmhouse my grandparents still lived in. The two houses sat on seventy-five acres of grass and wooded area. I saw deer, foxes, ground-hogs, random cats, and the occasional turkey on a daily basis. The stars in the sky were endless, and the sound of crickets and birds filled the evening breeze. I didn't realize how peaceful it was until I moved to a city and was introduced to smog and incessant car horn honking.

My town was small, but neighbors and schools were far away. It took a twenty-minute drive on one road, with very few cars and no traffic lights, to get to my high school. Growing up, I didn't pay attention to how "small-town middle America" it really was. It was my home, and it was all I knew. I graduated in 1998 with fifty-seven classmates, from a school that needed a lot of repairs, but had the best gymnasium I have ever been in (where I spent most of my time with a basketball on an old wooden floor). We took pride in our school, even though I didn't feel I got a great education. I loved sports and my heart belonged to basketball.

One morning during my Selfish Hour, I triggered a memory from fifth grade that hit me hard. What is really crazy is that I don't remember having thought about it since it happened, and yet I remembered every detail clearly as if it had happened yesterday. I pictured the classroom where I sat, how I felt... I could see every-thing. Mrs. Hoffman was my fifth-grade teacher during Desert Storm and our windows were plastered with yellow ribbons to show our support to all who drove by the school. My class had just come in from recess, and we were sitting at our wooden desks that had storage for books under the seat. Math came after recess, so I got my book ready.

Another teacher walked into our room and asked, "May I please see Megan?" I remember thinking, *Yay, I was specifically picked to get out of class for something cool.* At that time in my life, I didn't have any reason to think it could be anything else, but now if someone pulls me out of a meeting I assume the worst.

This teacher took me to a small room with a round table and asked me to sit down. I did as she asked, eagerly awaiting her to tell me about the cool project she needed my assistance on. Instead, she gave me a book and asked me to read some of the lines. I was confused but obliged. The sentences she asked me to read had a lot of S sounds. I read the sentences and then waited for her to say, "Gotcha, here is the fun project we are really gonna work on." But that never happened. I read more, and then she escorted me back to class. I had no idea what had happened. I only knew I was very disappointed.

Two days later, the same teacher came back again after recess and pulled me out of class to read more sentences, but this time she started to correct how I said the Ss.

I finally had the courage to ask her, "Why am I here?" I don't know if the teaching method in the eighties was to not tell students what was going on, but no one volunteered the information.

She replied, "You say your Ss with a lisp, and I am going to help you fix it." It was at that moment I realized I was in speech therapy. What's funny is I don't remember ever having a talk with my parents about speech therapy... even to this day. (Mom, if you read this can we finally talk about why you waited until fifth grade to address my lisp; just curious?)

A few weeks later, a different teacher named Miss Lundy came to our classroom and asked me to follow her out of class and bring my reading book. That time I went begrudgingly. I followed her down the hall, with my reading book held at my side, and up a set of stairs to a room that was the size of a small narrow bedroom. There were desks against one side of the wall, and there was barely enough room to walk past when someone was sitting.

I sat down with my book and a snarky attitude, and quickly asked, "Why am I here?"

She replied, "We are going to work on your reading skills."

At that moment I remember feeling different than all my friends; I felt like a bad kid. In my mind I didn't know anything was wrong with my reading, but I was placed in a special reading class to work on my speed and pronunciation. At eleven years-old, I felt that I wasn't as good as my friends; I felt not enough. I felt stupid. And so began my *story*.

On the bus ride home, I thought about all the Ss I had to say in speech therapy, and about being pulled from my classmates to get help with reading, and I couldn't help but feel like something was wrong with me. I felt sorry for myself, and I didn't want to share how I felt with my mom or anyone. When I got home, I bottled up my feelings and pretended as if everything was fine. Like it was just another normal school day. I didn't realize until I was thirty-five years-old that I created a story that molded into a belief that would be the underlying foundation for my life: the story of *"I am stupid."*

All these years I thought I was stupid, because I went to a bad school and received a poor education, which was not the case. I had no idea I created this reality for myself because of the thought *I am stupid*. Two teachers were doing their jobs and trying to make me better, but instead *I* made it mean I'm not smart.

For years my mother would question why I didn't bring any books home or have homework. I was always quick to answer that I finished it in school—which was a lie. I thought, *What's the use. I'm not smart anyway, so why try?*

My mom bought a video series called, *Where There's a Will, There's an A,* and she made me watch it on Saturday mornings. She had my aunt, whom I admired and was a successful educator, come and talk to me, but nothing penetrated my deep belief about my stupidity.

I felt everyone was wasting their time. I hated that my mom and aunt tried to make me better when they didn't understand that I was stupid and would never be able to learn. By high school, my story had been unconsciously upgraded from just a thought about myself to a fact in my mind: I am stupid.

Conversations in a Cadillac

" The happiness of your life depends upon the quality of your thoughts.

— Marcus Aurelius

HAVING MY EYES OPENED TO HOW I'D INCORPORATED THE *I AM stupid* story into my beliefs only made me want to know more. What other stories had I created? What was real, and what was made up? I was confused, curious, and eager to figure out more. My Selfish Hour took on more meaning. My meditation practice grew, and I learned breathing techniques to quiet my mind chatter so I could receive more insight into my past and myself. I found myself meditating at different times throughout the day just to gain more clarity and ground myself.

Through my journaling more things started to unfold, such as why I chose to be in certain relationships, and why I had some anger buried below my thoughts. Oftentimes, it felt like my fingers had minds of their own, and I wasn't the person typing. Words just flew out of me as if being guided. It was such a peaceful and powerful exercise, sometimes I would write something and have to pause because I had to acknowledge what just came out of me onto the page. When writing, I felt as if I was having a conversation with my subconscious. I asked myself questions, got quiet, and listened for the answer. I called this practice "Daily Conversations with Myself," and it included questions like:

- Why do I feel this way?
- Why? What's the real reason?
- What am I scared of other people knowing?
- What feelings and emotions are coming up for me today?

I just typed. It was a very therapeutic and exhausting activity. I almost didn't want to know why I do or think certain things, but my curiosity was sparked, and there was no putting out the flame.

One of those exercises had me relive a memory from ninth grade when I had my first high school basketball game. My mom and I pulled up to the school in her gray Cadillac Fleetwood. She and my dad thought it made them look rich and sophisticated, but it completely embarrassed me. It was the mid-nineteen nineties, I was fourteen, and my parents had a car so long that you couldn't hear the conversation in the front when you sat in the back. That thing was a beast, and my mom would purposely try to embarrass me by laying on the horn when the cute boys were outside, forcing me to bury my head in the seat screaming, "Knock it off, Mom! They will see me."

She put the car in park while I grabbed my bags, and, as I was about to get out, she said in her loving mother tone, "Megan, we are so proud of you and can't wait to watch you play tonight. Do your best, hustle, and try to score ten points."

My mother was a saint, and I know she had the best of intentions with her statement. However, what I heard was, "If I don't score at least ten points, I will be a disappointment to my family." What if I couldn't live up to the expectations she had for me? I didn't want to disappoint my mom.

Sitting in my Selfish Hour remembering this, I sank back in my chair, took a deep breath, and had a "holy shit" moment with my head in my hands. It felt like I was an outsider watching my life as a movie in fast forward. I could see myself in fifth grade, ninth grade, college, my career, relationships, and marriage. Everything started to make sense. Choices I made, people in my life, how I thought and felt about people and situations. From that moment on, I viewed my life from a completely different perspective. I realized that one person's intention and another person's perception of that intention could be completely different.

Starting in the ninth grade, two stories ruled my life. Story 1: I'm stupid, and Story 2: I need to overachieve. Of course, at that time I did not realize these were stories, that was my life...everything I knew. Feeling that way was in my DNA.

There were big glaring issues with these two stories in my mind: they butted heads. How can I overachieve if I am not smart? Only the smartest people overachieve, right? That realization helped me to put meaning to the unspoken internal struggle I always had but honestly didn't realize was a struggle. Again, I just thought it was who I was.

THE VAULT TO MY MEMORIES HAD BEEN UNLOCKED, AND conversations and situations began to emerge. One memory of a conversation helped me better understand my adolescent years. When I got injured my senior year of high school, and my dreams of playing basketball in college slipped away, I took a different route and became a model. I was five feet ten inches tall, gifted with good genes, and people told me I was pretty. While walking through the aisles of Big Lots chatting with my cousin, I said, "Since I'm not playing basketball, I'm going to become a model, because I'm not smart enough to do anything else." This statement didn't seem strange; rather, it simply seemed like the only other option I had.

With my core story of *I am Stupid* leading my life, I didn't apply myself in high school, and my grades reflected it. This caused my mom a lot of stress, while causing a lot of tension between us, but I was a teenager who thought playing sports or being a model were the only options available to me.

Light bulbs went off all over at 6:30 a.m. that morning. I began to understand myself. I could see how I viewed the world, the basis of my decision making, and how it led me to that moment. It is so fascinating how our minds work! It is a bottomless pit that stores a ton of information, and when you are ready to receive, it opens up and releases answers to questions you didn't even know you asked.

When the Music Stops

> **Beware of how you talk to yourself because you are always listening.**
>
> — Anonymous

AFTER GRADUATING HIGH SCHOOL, I ENROLLED IN YOUNGSTOWN State University (YSU), where most people in my family and around our area attended. I was so lost at this point in my life (I mean who isn't a little lost when they are eighteen years-old and their high school guidance counselor told them to figure out what they wanted to do with the rest of their lives?), believing that I wasn't smart and couldn't read well. One of the classes I took my first semester was an intro to college reading...basically, how to speed read to help get through textbooks faster.

I started as an engineering major, because my brother told me female engineers were in high demand and made a lot of money. This choice didn't work with Story 1 but aligned with Story 2. I went to one class and immediately walked into my student advisor's office and changed my major to business. I was still clueless about what I wanted to do, but I felt business left the door open to more suitable possibilities, and I didn't have to tell you how much water pressure was needed on floor nine of the hotel when someone on floor six took a shower.

My experience at YSU ended abruptly a year and a half in when I followed my heart and pursued a modeling career. Alongside going to college, and trying to figure out who I wanted to be when I grew up, I participated in beauty pageants. It all started when I was sixteen and entered into our local town festival beauty pageant and won, which led to county, state, and national pageants. I quite enjoyed pageant life, but kept this secret from my girlfriends for fear of being judged—that is until it all came out in our local paper. And then teenage mean girls came out.

I held the title of Miss Trumbull County, and while competing at the national level in Orlando, Florida, in 1999, I won "Most Promising Model" and was awarded a modeling scholarship. This award reinforced my thoughts that modeling was the path for me, because it was a career based on looks not smarts. The closest modeling agency to Ohio was in Philadelphia, Pennsylvania. I told my parents I wasn't even going to bother entertaining the scholarship, I didn't want to go to Philly. Back in those days I was a product of my environment, which meant I was cynical, negative, and focused on problems not solutions. (Apparently, I put on a good face during the beauty pageant and interview, so maybe I should have pursued an acting career.)

My mom pleaded with me to at least call the agency in Philly. So, to get her off my back, I picked up the puke green corded wall phone, dialed, and spoke to the owner of the agency. He invited my parents and me to come for a visit and see their agency. Two weeks later, we loaded up the car and headed east. We were simple country folks, and going to a big city in our beastly Cadillac was an adventure to say the least. My dad cursed at every passing car that came too close or was driving too fast, while my mother navigated from an atlas. I remember looking out the window in amazement at the skyscrapers, the pigeons eating crumbs off the ground, and the chaos of everyone walking fast and seeming very important, which was a completely different world from my seventy-five-acre farm. We got to the agency, where the owner was expecting us and escorted us into a tiny office that was plastered with pictures of famous models with their arms around him. He spoke to us about a big event, called the Model Association of America International (MAAI), scheduled two months from then in New York City. It was one of the biggest modeling events of the year, and a great place to be discovered. I felt so excited that my parents and I agreed that I would go and give it a shot. My plan of wanting to be a model because I wasn't smart enough to do anything else unfolded beautifully. I felt like that modeling event was the beginning of my journey.

My parents didn't have the time or the finances to make the six-hour trek to Philadelphia every weekend so I could prepare for the event. Instead, every Friday for two months, I took the overnight Greyhound bus which left Pittsburgh at 11 p.m. and got to Philly at 7 a.m., so I could get to the agency by 9 a.m. If you have never been on a Greyhound bus, please allow me to paint a picture. It smelled, it was scary, people carried their belongings in plastic bags, and I felt certain someone would rob me so I didn't blink for eight hours and gripped my duffle bag tightly on my lap.

Once I arrived in Philly, I went to a Dunkin Donuts (because there is one on every corner) where I pulled out my toothbrush and drug store makeup to make myself look presentable. At that time, I understood nothing about nutrition, so I grabbed a bagel with cream cheese, because in my mind that was a healthier option than a donut. Then off I went to modeling school.

I can still remember the look on the face of the director who sat at the front desk when I walked in on that first Saturday. I was chomping gum to cover up my bagel breath and I let the door slam behind me. It was like a movie when the music stops and everyone looks at the person who just walked in. There I was smelling like Greyhound bus funk, wearing a smile, and trying not to show how out of place I felt. Without saying a word, the director walked over with a tissue and a trash can, pointed to my mouth, and then at the can. After I had placed my gum in the tissue and thrown it away, she walked me over to the door in silence, opened it, put my hand on the knob, and showed me how to shut it properly so it wouldn't slam. Twenty plus years later and I still do not chew gum nor once has a door slammed behind me when I enter a room. A big etiquette lesson was received that spring morning.

Over the next two months, the agency put me through social grace classes: walking with a book on my head, getting in and out of a car like a lady, table etiquette, and how to walk up and down stairs in high heels and a skirt. I worked on a monologue and had a professional photoshoot in New York City with Frank Otten. I loved every second of it, because I felt I was able to be a new version of Megan, while I was in Philly working on my catwalk turns. Bye bye, country girl; hello, big city model.

Before I knew it, I arrived at the Waldorf Astoria Hotel in Manhattan for the MAAI weekend. Just being there felt like an out of body experience. I was like a little kid on Christmas morning chirping with joyful shrills, while my face was plastered with a huge smile, and my eyes were wide with wonderment. I had zero expectations for the event. I was content with being a participant. The weekend consisted of acting in a television commercial, reading a script with a soap opera actor, getting my headshots judged, and the big one: walking the catwalk.

Strutting my stuff down the runway, with the judges at the end critiquing my every move and swish was a moment I had prepared for. I had practiced my turns, my posture was confident, and I felt like Cindy Crawford. The thumping techno music filled the breathtaking high-ceiling ballroom with lights so bright, you couldn't see from the stage, so knowing how many people were in the room was a total guess. I watched the girl in front of me do her thing on the catwalk. Then it was my turn. I took a deep breath and began walking for every small-town country girl who wishes for an opportunity like that. I had taken only two steps onto the stage that looked a mile long when the music stopped. Dead silence. The silence was deafening, and I could hear whispers of people saying, "She doesn't have music."

I'm sure the judges would have been fine with me starting over once the music was corrected but I never broke stride. It was my time; my opportunity. I didn't need music. I didn't need the conditions to be perfect. I was so rehearsed that I did my walk, I smiled, and then gave a smoldering face as I looked one of the judges in the eye and did a sassy turn and walked back down the runway. At that moment, a new Megan was born. When I walked off the stage, I realized the whole place, including the judges, were clapping, because silence and posture are more powerful than loud music.

THE LAST DAY OF THE MAAI EVENT WAS THE AWARDS ceremony. I felt like I had already done my job and my work was behind me, so I didn't even know or really care what awards they gave out. I mean there were two thousand girls there from all over the world including Iceland, Greece, and Guam. This little country girl was just excited to be in NYC, walk the catwalk, meet new and interesting people, and try sushi and fumble with chopsticks for the first time.

Our agency's name was announced over and over, and my new friends were gracing the stage while I cheered loudly and witnessed the beginning of their careers. My hands hurt from clapping, and my voice was scratchy from hooting and hollering as a country gal does. The last award of the night was the Grand Overall Model, which is the person whose overall score was the highest. I was sitting in the mezzanine section in a floor length red dress that I borrowed from my cousin's girlfriend, and I prepped my camera to take a picture of the girl who was about to have her life changed forever.

Richard Bey was the announcer (I didn't know who he was, but my mom and aunts thought he was cool). He said, "The Grand

Overall Model from the John Robert Powers Agency in Philadelphia is Megan Phillips," but he pronounced my name *Meeee*-gan not Meg-an. I didn't know I had won until I was tackled by everyone sitting around me as they started to shove me toward the stairs so I could make my way to the stage.

I had no idea what I had won, or how my life was about to change. Matter of fact, when I walked on stage to accept my award, all the pictures of me look like a deer caught in headlights. I was happy and smiling but not even sure why I was happy other than that they called my name. After a few pictures on stage, the award ceremony was over, and I was left standing there while people were hustling and bustling about.

As I walked off stage, one of my teachers from the agency (who to this day is still my bestie) grabbed me and said, "Do you realize what you just won? Out of two thousand girls here you are the best one." I will never forget that moment and can still hear her voice and picture in my mind exactly where we were standing.

Her words put things into perspective, and my knees buckled as the tears started to wet my cheeks; I was laugh-crying and screaming, "What?!"

I had trained to walk on the runway and do a television commercial, but no one had trained me for what came next. As I tried to pull myself together, someone came over to me and said, "Don't go anywhere, the agent from Tokyo, Japan, wants to meet with you."

I recall looking at them completely startled and muttering, "Okay" then insecurity rushed through my veins and I thought, *I'm not skinny enough for that.* I was blinded by camera flashes while unknown faces hugged me with congratulatory wishes. In hindsight, I'm glad I didn't know what was ahead of me, because I probably wouldn't have left my small, safe cocoon I had built in Ohio, but deep down I knew this was exactly the path that I was supposed to take. My soul spoke to me and, instead of facing the unknown with fear, I was ready to take a risk, travel, and start something new with complete uncertainty of what was to come.

Within a few days, I flew back to Ohio, and my family threw me a big "you are onto bigger and better things" party. My mom and dad drove me to Philadelphia and dropped me off to start my new life. I can remember thinking that move would be the start of a new me, and it was in many ways, but what I realize now is that my stories packed their bags and moved from Northeast Ohio to the City of Brotherly Love. I remember thinking that if I just change my surroundings and circumstances, I will get to be the Megan who walked the catwalk. Many years later, I understood geographical changes do not change your internal thoughts and beliefs.

Video Game Villains

> Happiness does not depend on what you have or who
> you are. It solely relies on what you think.
>
> — Buddha

My early twenties were such an adventurous phase. I lived in downtown Philadelphia working as a model, attended college at Drexel University, and met people who were completely different from the ones I grew up around. I felt out of place but fully embraced the unknown. Picture me as basically a brunette version of Ellie Mae Clampett, from the 1960s television show *The Beverly Hillbillies*, without oil money, but with long legs, sharp features, and a quick personality to carry me through.

That chapter of my life resembled a video game. I was a young woman trying to find her way and do her best to move from scene to scene without getting swallowed up by villains. The villains had great disguises. One came in the form of my agents, who would weigh and measure me every Friday looking for decreasing numbers. My healthy body is a size six, but by living on salads, fat-free Cool Whip, and vodka with sparkling water, I shrunk myself to a size two.

Another villain was the homeless man I offered my uneaten snack to, only to have it thrown back at me while he shouted, "I don't want your food. I need money."

More villains were horrible dates and meaningless relationships, sleazy people who cared more about themselves; fraternity brothers that slipped my best friend and I roofies, and, of course, my corporate career was a big, scary villain dressed up as success. Villains were everywhere, but I didn't see them for what they were.

There was one villain who had the most impact on me, never left me alone, followed me everywhere, and always showed up when I was low or having a weak moment. It was the biggest, scariest, most powerful villain: my mind. More specifically, the villain was my thoughts.

This breakthrough realization came to me in the moments of an early morning Selfish Hour. I couldn't shake the thought, *I am the villain... my thoughts are the villain... I do this to myself.* At that moment, I took full responsibility for myself, for my life, and for all the decisions I had made. I stopped blaming others, I stopped pointing fingers, and I stopped being a victim of circumstances. I had won some battles against the villain, and she had won plenty against me.

The clarity I found that particular morning was so powerful that it was an unfamiliar feeling, yet it left me at peace. I realized I was in control of my thoughts, and my choices, and I could choose differently. I could choose to think and believe different thoughts about myself. This shift sounds like such a simple concept, but if you truly grasp what it means and practice thinking this way, you can genuinely change your life. Up to that day, my thoughts played the role of Super Mega Villain. I felt I had just learned the secret code to unlimited extra lives in the video game of my life.

My Selfish Hour lasted longer that day, as I felt as if I was looking into a crystal ball and seeing my life. The pieces of the puzzle finally came together.

The Space Between

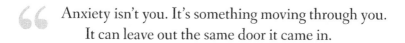
Anxiety isn't you. It's something moving through you.
It can leave out the same door it came in.

— James Clear

ARE THERE SONGS THAT YOU KNOW WHERE YOU CAN SING EVERY word by heart but not really understand the meaning? Then one day you hear the words, I mean actually hear the message the artist is expressing, and you can feel the pain or the emotion behind it? Those who grew up in the 1990s and 2000s probably know Dave Matthews and have likely been to a concert or two. I have been to several of his concerts, bought many of his CDs, and could sing along to countless songs.

One day, I was driving along and belting out the words like I was the lead singer while drumming on my steering wheel. I put on an awesome concert for myself. The song of choice was *The Space Between,* but this time, instead of just singing the words freely, my soul actually heard them. I can only presume that my mind was so open to receiving that I allowed myself to really *feel* the music.

It hit me like a Mack truck...the space between my stories of *I am stupid* and *the need to overachieve* was a sour feeling in my gut, a feeling that awkwardly became a safe place of comfort, a feeling that I had lived with for so long that it was part of me. The wicked lies of my stories kept me safe from pain, and became a space where I would smile and hide. The space between was anxiety.

I have anxiety. At thirty-six years old, I realized I had spent the greater portion of my life unknowingly swimming in anxiety. It made so much sense. I finally had a label for the feelings that had been with me since high school: feelings of fear, the inability to set aside worry, lack of concentration, and restlessness.

I felt like I had just won a freaking Grammy and was giving my acceptance speech. "I want to thank my loving husband Nick for questioning why I act the way I do. I want to thank myself for all the hard work I have done on my mindset. I want to thank Oprah for her guidance. I want to thank all the random people that led guided meditations, and, of course, Dave Matthews for a song that finally helped me to understand myself. This is such an honor. Thank you all for this award."

Anxiety is a word that I feel is thrown around too easily. I hear people say, "Oh, I can't do that. It gives me anxiety." Anxiety is intense. I had it so severely at times, I wouldn't drive a car because I didn't trust myself not to crash it. I didn't want to seriously injure myself, but just to shift the attention from the feelings in my gut, and the noise in my mind to something different.

I know this may sound crazy, but I can remember specific instances where I had to be somewhere, and I couldn't bring myself to start the car. It was truly a Jesus take the wheel type moment. Anxiety would also get the best of me in airports. I felt my legs stop working, and my heart racing, but I talked myself into pushing through. To numb my anxiousness, I stopped for a quick drink at an airport pub which allowed me to proceed with the flight. If I was traveling with someone, I hid how I felt for fear of being judged and embarrassed, but mainly because I didn't understand what was going on myself.

Once you put a label on something you can then take away its power. I'm not at all saying my anxiety is gone, but I now understand what I am feeling and know the tools to help me heal.

Life has a funny way of coming full circle. As I wrote this, I glanced at my office wall and saw a framed album cover signed by Dave when I met him backstage at one of his concerts in 2002. I got to hug him, he called me "pretty," and many years later his words led to my biggest breakthrough.

The Break-Up

 I am in a glass case of emotion.

— Will Farrell in *Anchorman*

AT THIS POINT IN MY JOURNEY, I GOT EXCELLENT AT ASKING THE right questions. *The Space Between* gave me all kinds of new questions and thoughts to ponder during My Selfish Hour, but one question that I needed to answer stood out with bright lights: "What had I done for more than twenty years to deal with my anxiety?" My thinking was short lived because the answers were glaring. I had two forms of self-medicating: exercise and alcohol helped me control my feelings—or so I thought. To me, having a knot in my stomach was part of my normal operating system. I referred to it as nervous energy. I came to find out that nervous energy is a first cousin to anxiety.

I rose early each morning, headed to the gym, got my sweat on, showered, and went to work. After work, I stopped at the bar with friends, shared laughs over numerous drinks, and decompressed after the day. This seemed like a totally normal and functional way of living. Many people did it and I was no different. Exercise gave me an endorphin rush to start my day, and alcohol helped me numb it at the end. On the outside, everything looked great. I excelled at my career, had a close circle of friends, and drove a sports car while wearing designer sunglasses. I thought the system I had unconsciously created was a well-oiled machine.

But have you ever stopped and looked at your life and thought that, if you took a picture of your outside and inside worlds and held them side by side, no one would see that they went together? Think of colors. The outside picture would consist of vibrant colors like yellow, pink, orange, green, and the color of the sky on a perfect summer day. But the inside image would look like the muddy color of the water after the paint brushes have been rinsed off. It is usually a dark brown/blackish color with a hue of nasty green. That is how my life felt at that time. My insides did not match my outsides, but I did my best to blend the colors with free weights, cardio classes, and Stoli vodka.

My self-diagnosed nervous energy was constant. I headed to the gym by 5:30 a.m. each morning and could not wait until my final work call was done so I could have a drink and calm my nerves. Even though I would stay out late while often saying, "I'll have just one more drink," I woke up early the next day to get my work out done and try to erase the night before. I tricked myself into thinking that my life was on track, when all I felt was emptiness and sour anxiety inside. I would go out Sunday to Thursday, because Friday and Saturday nights were when everyone wanted to go out, and I didn't like the crowds, or waiting for a drink. It didn't help that I lived above a bar and within walking distance to many of my favorite spots. Most of my friends were bartenders, so I felt like I was hanging out with them while they worked, and I drank with a friendly, inexpensive tab. I took pride in doing a blind fold test to easily identify the smell and taste of five different vodka brands to impress a bar of faceless locals on a Monday night. The fact that I made it through this chapter of my life unscathed is a direct sign that God had bigger plans for me.

At twenty-four years old, upon returning from a trip to Ohio to visit my family, I went out for a few drinks to shake off the six-hour drive, and I had one, or rather several, too many. When I came home from the bar, I stood in front of my bathroom mirror, my hands gripping the corner of the sink, and I couldn't recognize the person staring back at me. I didn't see the small town farm girl, I didn't see the model who walked the catwalk, I didn't see what other people saw. My mind jumped into full villain mode and feasted on that moment like a vulture on roadkill. I didn't know who I was, I felt lost, alone, and scared. I felt worthless and moved through life with no purpose or direction. I felt I was disappointing everyone, including God, who had given me special talents that went unused.

I didn't talk to my family much, because I was embarrassed that I was not the superstar model I set out to be. I pulled away from my friends because nothing felt right, and I blamed it on working a lot. My smile was fake, my laughter wasn't authentic, I wanted to be alone and avoided any deep conversation. I had an overwhelming sense of knowing what I had to do but not wanting to do it. I had bottled up my feelings for so long that I needed to figure myself out without my good friend Stoli. I had delayed facing this decision as long as I could, until one morning my boss and I were going to meet a potential client, and I couldn't keep up the act anymore. We got into my car, and I chugged coffee to cover up the aroma of alcohol from the night before.

My boss asked me for a folder with the background of the client we were meeting with, so he could bring himself up to speed before the appointment.

I looked at him and said, "I don't have it. I didn't even do it. I'm a fucked-up person and I need help. I can't do this anymore."

He looked at me with confusion, because I had been someone who appeared to have my shit together that he could count on.

I said, "I think I have a drinking problem."

I hit the pause button on life, took a break from my circle of friends, put myself in Alcoholics Anonymous (AA), and found a good therapist. I knew myself; I wasn't strong enough to be around my friends and not drink. I had a conversation with my boss and told him my plan. Since he was one of my drinking buddies with a huge heart, he decided to "let me go" so I could collect unemployment and focus on my health. Leaving my job and severing the connection with my friends were extreme measures, but I knew that I needed to do both to get my life straight.

I remember googling AA meetings near me and feeling like a failure. AA was awkward, and I didn't feel like I fit in. I walked into my first meeting scared and confused, but with a determined feeling to prove I wasn't meant to be there. The room was located in a random building that I drove past a million times but never knew was there.

When I entered the building, the greeter saw new blood and took to me. "Welcome, what's your name?"

I shyly answered while I looked around the room seeing if I randomly knew anyone, which I did not. There were cliques of people that I remember thinking I wouldn't be friends with. I saw everyone holding a Styrofoam cup of coffee, so I made my way over to the commercial-sized coffee pot and filled a cup. I nervously chugged it and immediately poured a second cup.

People kept trying to talk to the "new gal," but I didn't engage much; I just wanted to be a wall flower and observe. I hated introducing myself as, "Hi, I'm Megan and I'm an alcoholic."

I listened to people's stories but kept thinking I couldn't relate. I didn't wreck a car or relationship, and my boss wouldn't have known if I hadn't told him that I thought I was drinking too much. All of my friends were at the bar right then drinking and probably wondering where I was, so why was I sitting in that room filled with random faces, drinking mediocre coffee, and claiming my identity? I was a ball of confusion.

I didn't feel I could function right in society, and I didn't feel like I fit within the walls of an AA room. Despite hating everything at that moment, I pushed through and kept showing up to focus on me, and not on the interesting collection of people in my new world. I did eventually find friends inside AA with whom I would go out to dinner with after a meeting. I hired a therapist because I was desperate and determined to change myself. The overachiever in me wanted to win this new battle. I never realized the amount of baggage I had packed away and moved from Ohio to Philadelphia, but it started to unpack its nasty self whether I wanted to or not.

I chose an AA sponsor who also ran a house cleaning business. I began working for her to make extra cash alongside my unemployment. My daily routine was completely different from the gym-work-bar routine I had created years ago. I began each day with a 7 a.m. AA meeting, then I picked up cleaning supplies, got the addresses of houses to clean, and got busy doing just that.

I vividly remember scrubbing a bathroom in a beautiful mainline mansion in the suburbs of Philadelphia. The mainline is an expensive and beautiful area where old money, expensive cars, and trust fund kids typically live. And there was me, in dirty clothes, with Clorox, cleaning a house I believed deep down I should be living in.

One night, I dreamed that I drove my sports car home to my mansion and inside were people cleaning my house. As I walked through the house, which I had paid for from my own success, I was full of joy and laughter. I plopped myself onto the plush couch in the living room and saw a copy of a book I had written on the coffee table. When I woke up the next morning, I had hope in my heart for the first time in a long time. I knew my position in life was a test, and this humbling experience was building me. I needed to create a new version of me to get through it.

I SPENT SIX MONTHS ALCOHOL FREE, GIVING MYSELF THE opportunity to understand who I was without the influence of other people or liquid courage. My life had been about moving from one scene to the next so quickly, fighting off villains that I never took time to process, that I didn't even think about my thoughts and feelings. Honestly, I never knew that was even a thing.

Spending quality time with myself when I had avoided it for so many years was a challenging thing to do: hearing my thoughts, analyzing them, and deeply feeling the emotions I had worked so hard to avoid. As Will Farrell said in *Anchorman*, "I was in a glass case of emotion" and didn't know how to get out.

During my sober period, I turned to my dad's sister, Aunt Helen, who I had always admired, and who was the only family member that I could talk openly with. To me, she was the smartest and most worldly person I knew, who also understood me and the inner workings of my family. She grew up in the farmhouse next to my parents' house, and she got out of Ohio just like I had. She was the type of person who could listen, think, and give an intelligent response. Unlike with most people I knew, who already had an opinion they were waiting for an opportunity to share, I valued each word she said —and I still do.

When I called her and explained that I was in AA and cleaning houses, she calmly but very frankly said something that forever changed me. She wanted me to address the bigger, underlying issues that had never been discussed in my twenty-four years of life.

She said, "The first thing you need to understand is that your dad is a functioning alcoholic."

When I heard these words, I sat there dumbfounded. What? How was that even possible? I mean, sure he drank every day. Yes, I had seen him passed out. Yes, he liked to have a good time, but wasn't that just being a country boy? Where I grew up, people took pride in drinking. It's just what was done. You worked hard at your labor job, you worked in the yard, you fixed cars in the garage, while your good friends Miller, Bud, and Coors hung out with you in support.

That wasn't how all parents did it? was a brand-new thought that made me feel naïve. How had I not realized something that, once spoken, seemed so obvious?

At that moment, I understood my definition of normalcy was completely skewed. This knowledge sent a shockwave through my whole sense of reality. I was college educated, I was accomplished, and I had moved away from my parents and lived on my own. How had I not realized this truth?

Having a beer was *not* the preferred drink with dinner for every man in America?

I thought the people who didn't do that were odd, not the other way around. This new information really came as a shock. I admired my dad. He could fix anything, he would be there to help anyone who needed him, and he fished and hunted. He was my dad, and he was an alcoholic. Even though I was the one in AA saying, "Hi my name is Megan and I'm an alcoholic," it was hard to see my dad in this light. Every AA meeting I attended, I didn't quite identify with being an alcoholic. I did come to understand that I am an adult child of an alcoholic. I love my dad but not his choices.

My dad called me when I went into AA and said, "I think you need to move home. You obviously can't take care of yourself on your own."

I told him I would move home if he would quit drinking with me and we could do this together. I heard silence on the other end of the phone and a quick change of subject, and it was never spoken of again.

I researched Adult Child of Alcoholics (ACOA) and it was like reading a book about myself. It gave answers to questions I didn't even know I had. I read about impulsive behavior, isolation, not understanding what "normal" was, difficulty in romantic relation-ships, lack of positive coping mechanisms for managing stress, and perceived victimhood. Holy shit! I could give specific examples of me in each of those categories. Finally getting answers to under-stand feelings was both a sense of relief and major frustration. Labeling what I felt was a relief, but the overachiever in me felt frus-trated that I hadn't realized sooner and wanted to handle it yesterday.

Here was my new reality: I was an adult child of an alcoholic who hadn't learned how to cope with his disease or how it had affected me. I unconsciously repeated learned patterns. Yes, the disease ran through my blood, and I was on that path and could have easily continued, but, I had made a decision to change.

Talking about our feelings may have been a foreign concept in my childhood home, but I also wasn't aware that it was missing. I was never taught how to express myself in a healthy way. All I knew was how to press my emotions deep down and act like they didn't exist because that was what others around me did. Shouldn't this type of stuff be taught in school instead of algebra? Seriously, what do you need more in life: algebra or healthy emotional coping mechanisms? I think the scale tips heavily to one side.

Feelings, well that was a whole new thing that I discovered—actually feeling an emotion instead of suppressing it, pushing it away, or drowning it in alcohol. A flashback appeared in my mind of me sitting at the bar with friends and saying, "I drink when I'm happy, I drink when I'm mad, and I drink when I'm sad." Holy shit! I had used alcohol to escape feeling *any* emotion.

The next morning during my Selfish Hour, I released myself from the versions of me I created just to survive, and it was liberating!

The Therapist and the Patient

 If nothing changes, nothing changes.

— Anonymous

WHEN I WORKED IN THE CORPORATE WORLD, AT THE END OF every year it was a common practice to set goals for the upcoming year. For thirteen years, I routinely did this, but it felt like I was setting goals to please other people, and never setting goals for myself. The goals were usually based on numbers, money, and achievement. In 2017, while still working for "The Man," I attended a weekend-long business seminar led by a very good friend and mentor of mine, Bob Heilig. I had been at his house the week prior and knew he was offering a high-ticket, year-long mastermind coaching package at the end of the weekend. I also knew at that time there was no way I was going to join it because I couldn't afford the price tag.

At the end of the second day of Bob's seminar, he said something that had a profound impact on me. He said, "How long are you going to go on wanting things to change but not really doing anything about it?'

His question hit me like a Mike Tyson punch in the face. I realized that if nothing changed in my life, nothing would change. I wasn't exactly sure what I wanted *to change*; I just knew something needed to. That weekend, I went against everything I said I wouldn't do and made a huge financial and personal commitment by joining his year-long mastermind. At this time in life, I had a full-time career, a side business, two small kids, a husband who traveled a lot for work, and no family living close to help out. I dove in head first because I knew with every fiber of my being that was my next step. I was scared shitless to tell Nick what I wanted to invest, but luckily, he believed in me.

Nick's comment was, "Well we are already in debt, does it really matter how much? Just use the Southwest card to get some miles out of it."

Thank God he loved me and believed in me!

I was already full force with my Selfish Hours, working on my internal game. This new venture was the second layer I added. I surrounded myself with motivated business people and expected everything to unfold magically for me. I showed up for every Zoom training, flew across the country to live events, received one-on-one coaching to get my ideas picked apart, did all the homework assignments, and six months into the journey, didn't feel like I was getting anywhere. There was no lightbulb moment, I didn't have a brand, an idea, a vision, nada, nothing, zilch. I lived in faith that it would come to me, but I felt discouraged every time I gave the fake answer to my husband or friends when they would ask how the mastermind was going. "Oh, it's great. I'm learning so much." I fully embraced living with Imposter Syndrome and was pretty damn good at it.

One of our assignments was to create our goals for the upcoming year. I rolled my eyes at the fact I was again creating goals for someone else, but this time was different. The assignment wasn't focused on goal setting; it was on goal achievement, which until then I didn't realize was different. No numbers, no "how much money do you want to make this year?" The questions presented were different and made me think. The first one was: *Who do you need to be in order to call this your breakthrough year?* The next question that took me two days to answer was: *What do you need to let go of to become the person you want to be?* The difference with these questions was that the answers weren't about what you were going to *do*, but about who you were going to *be*—a complete departure from the goals I'd created in the past.

My initial thought was, *I need to let go of my fear of failure which is fueled by my need to overachieve,* but with my new zest for life I knew I needed to dig deeper. I reflected on my life and noticed the imbedded thought and behavioral patterns. One pattern that stuck out to me was that I had some level of success in whatever I focused on, but I didn't feel I had ever truly tapped into my potential, or pushed myself to see what I was really capable of.

When a contest would be presented at work such as the annual "win an all-expense paid trip to Cancun for you and your spouse, if you achieve these numbers over the next three months," I would speak encouraging words on the outside, but the words inside my head were always, *You won't win it so don't try, do just enough so it looks like you tried and just missed.* Each year, when I wouldn't hit the numbers to win the contest, I oddly felt justified in my mind because I didn't fully try. My thoughts sabotaged me out of some amazing experiences.

Growing up, I often heard my parents and other adult family members say that, as a Phillips (my maiden name), we don't win; it was easy for everyone else, but not us. We mess up and life tends to shit on us. Basically, everything is a *struggle.* Money was hard to come by and a struggle to keep. I didn't realize until I focused on the answer to the question about "what I needed to let go of" that I adopted this thought process as my own. As a competitive person, I love to compete. As I dug deeper, I realized that, yes, I loved competition, but I always expected to lose. Losing was a more comfortable space than winning.

People tend to think that because I was in sales, I was motivated by prizes and trips. However, I would never fully go for these rewards because I didn't expect to win. All these years I thought I had a fear of failure, but it was actually a fear of success, and I didn't feel worthy of winning. The deeper I dug into the abyss, the more questions I had.

Meditation helped me get to the bottom of what I needed to let go of, and the answer was a hard pill to swallow. The story of *struggle* wasn't mine. It was my father's story, given to him by his father, who grew up in the Great Depression when it *actually was* a struggle. Who knows how many generations back this belief goes. I wore this story like a custom-made jacket—and it wasn't even mine!

Damnit, I took on other people's stories and believed them as my own. This just opened up a whole new can of worms. That day, I became both the therapist and the patient.

Corporate Refugee

> Burn the boats as you enter the island and you will take the island.

— Napoleon Hill

IN OCTOBER 2017, SIX MONTHS INTO BOB HEILIG'S mastermind, I was preparing to take the stage as a keynote speaker at The Polka Dot Powerhouse Annual Celebration in Denver, Colorado. My forty-five-minute presentation was titled, "It's your Story." In it, I highlighted how our stories were a movie that played on repeat in our minds. I planned to share my own stories, and teach a room of three hundred women how to uncover their own. I had prepared for weeks and was ready to lead these women to a breakthrough. The night before the speech, I was in my room ready to rehearse and here was what that looked like: I donned my heels and slapped lipstick on, stood in front of the mirror, and delivered my presentation enthusiastically. I am my own biggest critic, so if I can give an impactful presentation to myself, I can make an impact on anyone.

I started to say, "Good morning and welcome, so excited to be here with you," and then my mind went blank. I had nothing. I shook it off and started over. "Good morning, beautiful ladies. I'm so excited to be here with you," and my mind became a big white screen again. I gave a quick glance at my notes, trying to stay calm, but the color left my face, my palms got sweaty, and my stomach had the all too familiar sour feeling come rushing in.

Anxiety came in hard and fast. What was I going to do? I forgot my whole presentation. Sure, I had it written down, but I couldn't stand up there and read it like the president giving the State of the Union address. This was not my first time speaking, so why did I feel a huge block in my mind? I wanted to throw up, I wanted to call my husband, crying, and say, "I'm not good enough to do this." My nerves had the best of me at that moment, the night before I was scheduled to be on stage wowing a crowd.

I pulled myself together and thought about what I could do. I remembered I had a great friend, Nicole, who was also attending the event. I went on a mission to find her. I found her eating dinner.

I said, "I need your help. Can we talk?"

Here's the thing about a great friend who gets you: there was no hesitation. She just replied, "Want to talk in your room?" She knew and understood my topic.

I explained I had some sort of block. She sat back and gave a laugh. I felt annoyed and small for her laughing at me as I paced around my room but I trusted her.

She said in a gentle, calming voice, "Your fifth-grade self is so present right now."

Huh? What? I stopped pacing and stared at her. My voice was sharp when I said, "What do you mean?"

She explained I was not operating from the present moment but rather from my fifth-grade story of *I am stupid*. I was self-sabotaging in full force.

I took a deep breath and shook my head in laughter because I couldn't believe I wasn't aware. "You are totally right!" I said.

Then she said something that gives me chills every time I think about it. "Here is why that is happening: your fifth-grade self is friends with all the other fifth graders who will be in that room tomorrow, and she is trying to protect them."

Even though that statement was heavy, it made me feel extremely light; as if a hundred pounds lifted from my shoulders. Within seconds, my entire speech came flooding back to me. I went to bed that night realizing I still had a lot of work to do around my stories. Step one was complete: I identified them, but my awareness still needed work.

I woke up the next morning feeling confident to take the stage. I loved my outfit, which was important as it added to my confidence thermometer. It's one thing to give a presentation and talk to people, but it's another to make people *feel* your words so they can create their own breakthrough and leave the room a different version of themselves. In the last ten minutes of my talk, something overtook me and I went in a completely different direction than I had intended.

I felt Oprah and God on my shoulder saying, "It's time and you are ready." I felt the feeling and went with it. I shared myself in a room full of three hundred women, some of whom were friends, some I knew from social media, and others were faces that blended in the background. I opened up a part of myself that only the inner five friends in my circle knew, and it was something that I had wanted to do for more than two years. I knew if I didn't share it, it may never happen.

I declared loudly with a little crackle in my voice, "Next month, I am going to quit my job. I am going to take control of my life, and follow the passion God placed in my heart and become a coach, so I can help all of you uncover the stories that are holding you back from your greatness. We are given one life, and if we live it with untapped potential in our hearts, that is not serving our purpose. I can't continue living a life that is no longer serving me. I am asking all of you to hold me accountable. I am done thinking about it, wishing for it, and writing it down. The time has come for me to take courageous action." I was talking, but the words were coming from my soul.

The crowd stood up and cheered as I stood on stage smiling with happy tears flowing down my face. My goal had been to give the crowd a personal breakthrough and it was me who had had one. I closed my presentation and through the cheers, I heard Alicia Keys' voice come through the sound system playing, *This Girl is on Fire.* It's a moment I will never forget.

I walked off stage smiling and waving, moved straight out of the ballroom and into the bathroom, shut the stall door, leaned on the wall, and cried. With my head in my hands, I thought *What the hell did I just do?* I understood getting an audience reaction, but telling everyone I would quit my thirteen-year career—what the fuck, Megan? My mind raced and thought of myriad ways to get out of following through. *Maybe no one would remember to hold me accountable?* And if they did, I would just tell them that I was caught up in the moment. But that made my stomach turn. If I didn't have my word, what else did I have?

Still leaning on the wall of the stall, I thought back to the plane ride that brought me from Philadelphia to Denver. Before I left home, I grabbed a notebook from my office. I liked to have something with me to take notes or write down ideas as my imagination flowed. Sitting on the plane, I pulled out the notebook and leafed through the pages. I read notes I had previously scripted and, no surprise, it was a gratitude journal. I loved reading about my dreams and what held a big place in my heart. Then I read something that caught my attention: "I am so grateful to quit my job on December 31, 2015."

As I continued to leaf through more pages, I saw another entry that made me close the book and put my head back and think. I don't know what it was about planes, but I do my best thinking in the air. Here is what I read: "I am so grateful I quit my job on December 31, 2016." It was October 2017, and I still worked in the same job. I leaned back on the headrest and closed my eyes. I thought of what it was going to take for me to leave my job. Hope had been my strategy, but that didn't seem to be working and, obviously, I didn't make big decisions on New Year's Eve. Could I really quit my job? Nick and I were buying a house in a few weeks and starting renovations. My oldest had just started kindergarten at a private school and my youngest was in daycare.

My mind only focused on ways me quitting wouldn't work, and why the timing was never going to be right. I knew the tools to bring my mindset back to the positive, but at that moment I only wanted to focus on the negative and how what I had declared was a bad move.

God had a different plan and knew I needed to do something bold, and that was why my declaration happened on stage. My soul stepped up to the plate. Timing would never be right, but when you live in faith, sometimes, you need to feel the fear and do it anyway. Our words have creative power. I walked on stage as one person that morning and walked out of the bathroom stall as another. A little over a month later, on November 16, 2017, I became a corporate refugee and never looked back.

The journey hasn't been easy nor inexpensive, but I have never felt more in alignment with my dharma.

People often ask me, "How did you do it? How did you walk away from your job when you were the main breadwinner of your family, knowing you were putting your family at risk?"

My answer is simple, "I know me, and I will do whatever it takes to make things happen. It may be tough at moments, but I know that is building my character and my story." I also knew if I had the safety net of the job, I would never fully give myself to a coaching business. I needed to burn the ships and pivot my life. You will amaze yourself when you eliminate all other options but one. You learn how to be the person you need to be in order to make the dream a reality.

Every time I wanted to give up or felt I wasn't enough, Nick was always there to pick me up. With one sentence, Nick could shift my focus. "Megan, it's all part of your story." Hence this book.

Let it Go

> I believe every single event in life that happens is an opportunity to choose love over fear.
>
> — Oprah Winfrey

THE DENVER TRIP WAS A PIVOTAL MOMENT IN MY JOURNEY. I realized how much my mindset had grown while also shining a light on how much more work there was to be done. The journey of self-development, of truly understanding myself, was really the greatest education I could get. It may have been free, but some of the lessons were hard to learn.

Next, I had to learn when my stories were present, and this question raced through my mind: *How do I get the stories to stop?* As much as I wanted it to be easy, I knew that I couldn't wave a magic wand and say, "Well, now I know my stories, so I'll just stop using them!" These stories have been with me for the greater part of my life, I couldn't trust that I could just change my beliefs. Naturally, the next question presented itself: *How do I change a belief?*

When I googled, *how to change a belief*, the first thing I read was,

"Changing a core belief is surprisingly easy. You simply stop believing in them."

Simply stop believing in them? Are you freaking kidding me? That made zero sense to me. I just proved in Colorado that I didn't even have an awareness of when beliefs showed up, how was I supposed to stop believing? Didn't Journey tell us to, *Don't Stop Believin'*?

I looked through the numerous books on my bookshelf and everything I read was, "How to let go of your limiting beliefs." Let go? Are you serious? That sounded impossible. How on earth did I let go of something that felt like a part of me? Nothing about these authors' writings resonated with me and I instantly felt defeated. But my new mode of operation was not to focus on the problem and instead find a solution. Okay, a solution. Then I googled, *what is the opposite of letting go?* The first three words I read were: *Retain. Hold tight.*

I felt completely conflicted. I didn't feel I could simply let go, but I didn't want to retain or hold tight to my beliefs either. This conflict played out in my head for days without clarity. Then one night, while watching *Frozen* for the millionth time with my daughters, I had an "ah-ha" moment and started laughing. In the blockbuster hit Elsa sung, "Let it go," but later realized love was the answer, and she knew how to control her gifted powers. Elsa was absolutely right: love is the answer. I didn't need to let go of my fifth-grade self, I needed to love her. I needed to give her an identity, acknowledge her, and build a relationship with the storm inside. Just like I experienced with the Dave Matthews song, I could hear something over and over, but then one day I heard the message completely differently, and it had a profound effect on me.

The next morning in my Selfish Hour, I knew I needed to give my fifth-grade self an identity so I could separate from her. I had heard my friend Nicole talk about her inner child and giving her a name, but I didn't truly understand what she meant until that moment.

I asked, What is your name?" I got quiet and listened for the answer. The first and only name that I heard was Myka, so that is what I wrote down. Giving my fifth-grade self a name felt a little like having an imaginary friend, but she is real, she is a part of me, she is fifth-grade me with a long-haired perm, bangs, neon clothes, snap bracelets, and a love for Vanilla Ice and New Kids on the Block. I felt her presence, and she made me feel warm, comfortable, and safe. She had always been there, but this was the first time I had acknowledged her as a separate identity.

During this Selfish Hour, I felt the pull to type out my thoughts because I needed to separate my ego from my intuition. My meditation practice had taught me to quiet the ego and tune into my inner source, and I knew Myka lived in my inner source. I wanted to get to know her and understand her role in my present life and why she continued to hang on.

After a lot of writing, I realized I could sum her up with one word: protector. She would come in with her sword and shield ready to protect me when she felt I might be viewed as stupid, and she held me back from sharing my opinions. She held me back when I wanted to stretch outside my comfort zone and try something new. She held me back to protect the other fifth graders from being revealed at the keynote speech in Colorado, and she was in the bathroom stall to think up an excuse to retract my declaration. She was my core red light story, which is a story we tell ourselves that holds us back, keeps us playing small, disguises as self-sabotage, and reinforces that we are not enough. A core red light story was the root that all other stories stemmed from. Myka paid me a visit every time I sat down to write this book.

She would say, "Who do you think you are? You aren't a writer; no one will read this. Your grammar is terrible. Remember you are stupid." Her voice was always there in my mind. She has not gone away, but I have learned how to put her to the side and get back to productive action within a few seconds.

Through my years, I have read countless self-development books and attended numerous seminars, but I never truly understood what people on stage or in the books meant by self-sabotage or playing small. No one ever talked to me about this before. No one told me to give my inner child an identity and counseled me to love her. Or maybe I just never found that book or speaker to help me with taming Myka. Maybe because it sounded like voodoo, maybe because it's not textbook; but to my mind, it was the only thing that made sense.

This is actually what self-sabotage means: you don't realize you are doing it until you understand the role your younger self is playing in your life. Myka feels she is protecting me, but what she is actually doing is keeping me small and sheltered. I will never live up to my God-given purpose if I am held back by the thoughts of my younger self driving my actions. I operated out of history and memory instead of vision and imagination. The clarity I experienced that morning was like looking at the most beautiful lake with a mountainous landscape backdrop on a crisp fall morning. Clarity for endless miles. I no longer felt small. I felt heard. Myka felt acknowledged that morning for the first time ever. From that moment on, I have loved her with compassion, which is all she ever wanted.

Even with this clarity, I still felt a heaviness inside of me. When she needed love the most, I gave her alcohol to drown her out, or I increased my weights at the gym trying to push her down.

I cried for her and I cried for me. She was just trying to protect me, and I tried to poison her. She was just a little girl. What you don't know, you don't know until you know, then you feel like shit.

I thought back to my six months of sobriety in my early twenties and was surprised I hadn't discovered Myka then, but I also don't think I was ready. I needed to grow more before my emotional state was ready to receive her message. I truly believe on this journey everything happened when it was supposed to. I didn't begin to emotionally develop until my mid-twenties so at thirty-five, when I did my second self-discovery journey through The Selfish Hour, I was really only ten or eleven years old emotionally. Interesting that when my emotional journey reached eleven years-old, I met my eleven-year-old self. Coincidence?

Who am I?

> Between stimulus and response there is a space, in that
> space is our power to choose our response. In our
> response lies our growth and our freedom.
>
> — Viktor Frankl in *A Man's Search for Meaning*

I CAN RECALL WHEN I WAS CREATING CONTENT FOR MY
business and tuned into the words swirling through my mind. *You
aren't good enough. Nothing you have to say has value. This post is
stupid. Everyone who reads this is going to unfollow you.* I was very
conscious of these thoughts and realized who was present. Myka was
in control of my mind.

I felt her presence and said, "Hey, Myka, thanks for showing up.
It's okay, we are safe, and I got this." Acknowledging her and letting
her know that adult Megan had this, allowed her to relax and leave,
so I could create. It was an oddly magical moment.

Creating awareness around my thoughts and feelings, instead of
just letting them happen was a huge awakening. For the first time in

my life, I felt I was not only understanding my mind but learning how to use it powerfully.

I glanced at a quote written on a Post-it note in my office, and in that moment it took on a deeper meaning. The quote was from Viktor Frankl's book *A Man's Search for Meaning*, "Between stimulus and response there is a space, in that space is our power to choose our response. In our response lies our growth and our freedom."

Learning to separate from Myka and choosing to respond from a new space was where growth and freedom began.

As with all my breakthroughs, new thoughts brought new questions. One question that played ping pong in my mind was, "If I wanted to separate from Myka, and chose to respond 'I got this,' who is the 'I' who has this?" *Who am I?* These three little words could make anyone sit back, take a deep breath, and ponder. If you asked me to write out all my flaws or areas that I needed to improve, I could give you a list of twenty in a few minutes, but listing out good qualities was much tougher.

I spent so much time getting clear on who Myka was, but the *Who is Megan?* question was a whole other level that I needed to tackle before the sun came up in this Selfish Hour. It was like being at a job interview and they asked, "What three words best describe you?" Why is this such a hard question to answer? We can juggle the house, kids, school and activities, make dinner, pay the bills, excel at our careers, volunteer, be a good friend; but, when asked what your superpower was, we can only mutter the words: "I don't know, I'm not really good at anything."

I forced myself to sit down and list out all my best qualities. I stared at a blank screen and wrote down a few things then erased them. Ugh, I was getting nowhere fast. To make it easier, I listed out what I thought Nick would say about me, then what my best friend would say, and then what my mom would say. It was easier to wrap my mind around what other people thought of me than what I thought of myself. I had a long list, and from the words written I circled the top ten that resonated with me. From the top ten, I reduced the list down to five. I wrote those five words on a Post-it note, and put it up in my office. I also had the list set as an alarm on my phone, so it would pop up during the day and remind me of who I am. This was the process I used to reprogram my brain to focus on the solutions and the positives rather than the problems and the negatives.

The most ironic part about the reprogramming was that several times the alarm went off when Myka was very present. I referenced this experience as a divine intervention and would look up to acknowledge where this sign came from and give a sincere, "Thank you. I'm getting it." Seeing my five words brought awareness to what was really happening. I would assess the situation, understand what triggered my fifth-grade insecure self to show up, smile, say out loud, "Thank you for showing up, but spirited, courageous, thoughtful, kind, magnetic Megan has this." This was literally how I learned to separate and reframe my past, day after day, and sometimes moment by moment.

People in my inner circle started to see a difference in me and asked what pills I was taking or what had happened to me? My response left them with a dumbfounded yet curious look as I said, with joy and confidence, "You can't change your past, but you can change your relationship to it, and that's what I did."

Part Two

The Detachment Method

> We need to forget what we think we are, so that we can
> really become what we are.

— Paulo Coelho

I ENJOYED THE PROCESS OF UNDERSTANDING MYKA AND
beginning to acknowledge when she was present in my life. She was
such a comfortable and safe part of my life; it was easy to disregard
my feelings when she was present. I still struggled with knowing
when she was present, and I often operated from a scarcity mindset.

I remember one time in particular, when my oldest daughter
Codi was in first grade, and she was learning the new common core
math, which was frustrating for anyone who grew up learning one
way of doing math only to have to relearn it all over again to be
supportive to their child.

I had helped Codi with her homework the night before, and it
came back with red marks on the page. We had the right answers but
didn't show the work the correct way. Myka basically took over my

body, and I felt so stupid that I couldn't do first grade math. I felt even lower that my seven-year-old thought her mom couldn't help her. It was as if the red pen came to life, jumped off the page, and did a big cartoon slap across my face.

Nick saw the marked-up homework page and, in a jovial voice, said, "Mommy, let's sit down and teach you, too."

Needless to say, I did not take to this very well, and if I had a smoke stack at the top of my head you would have seen and heard the steam erupting. I proceeded to fire back at him, "I already graduated. I don't need to learn math all over again."

He pointed out that he was about to enter baseball season and would not be home in the evenings, so I needed to understand new math so I could help Codi.

I reluctantly sat down next to him, feeling completely annoyed with matching body language, while he taught our seven-year-old, and me, first grade math. The rest of the night was ruined. I felt small, I felt stupid, and I felt he was surely judging me. This was a story I created. Nick never said anything more about it and neither did Codi. But in my mind, they were meeting up secretly and laughing at how dumb Mom was, and how she couldn't do math. Our mind is powerful and can get us to believe anything.

It wasn't until the next morning when I sat quiet in my Selfish Hour, that I realized exactly what had happened. Myka was in the driver seat of that conversation, and present-day Megan was in the backseat taking a nap. I needed to create a game plan to avoid her take-over of my reactions, so she couldn't cause a fight with Nick in front of our girls, and ruin our precious evenings together. I wanted to learn coping mechanisms to have a healthy emotional response to simple things like first grade freaking common core math.

In my next Selfish Hour, I still felt stupid and embarrassed over how I reacted. As I sat in silence and thought about how I could have handled the situation better, one word kept coming to mind: detach. I needed to learn how to detach myself from Myka. But how the hell could I have done that when I wore Myka like a

Halloween costume and wasn't even aware until the next morning?

I desperately wanted to change that part of me. I wanted to understand what it meant to respond and not react. Up until that point, I thought these two were synonymous. But a reaction is typically quick and can be a defense mechanism. A response, on the other hand, is thought out and non-threatening. A response takes into consideration the well-being of not only you but those around you. A reaction and response may look exactly alike, but they feel different.

That morning I created a simple three-step system I named The Detachment Method to teach myself how to respond and not react. The steps are:

- Awareness
- Separation
- Response

Step 1: Awareness

I wanted to become conscious of when Myka was present, fully aware and mindful of the voices in my head. Who was saying them? Myka, me, or an outside influence? Were they stories or fact? The only way to become aware is to be tuned into my thoughts and feelings.

The reason I say feelings is because as a woman I usually notice first how I am feeling and then back track the feelings to my thoughts. When I am feeling small, insecure, or uncertain, it's like a red flag to pay attention to my thoughts. What am I thinking that is leading me to *feel* this way? Many times, the thought would be: *I don't want to sound stupid,* or *your opinion isn't that important, and people will think your suggestion is dumb.* Of course, when you think these thoughts, the natural vibration in your body is going to be small, insecure, or uncertain.

Creating awareness of my thoughts and feelings was the starting point of change. When you are self-aware and fully present, you can see where your thoughts and emotions are guiding you. Learning how to become more present is the first step in creating the life you want.

I quickly came to the conclusion that with awareness comes responsibility; a responsibility to choose and act differently. This is actually the hardest part. I had to learn that when I felt mad, sad, hurt, anxious, ignored, disrespected, or whatever feeling it may be that would typically cause me to react, I must just stop. Stop talking, stop yelling, just stop in my tracks and assess what is happening. It was the only way I could think of to shift this.

Step 2: Separate

With this heightened sense of awareness and the ability to control my reaction, I needed to move to the next step: separation. When I want to react to Myka (my story), I must choose to separate myself from her. The word choice is powerful. We always have a choice, and most of the time we choose the comfortable, easy, knee jerk route which is typically to react. This is why having a separate identity for your story helps. You need to distinguish between the present day you and your story.

Step 3: Response

Once you have an awareness that you are triggered but have stopped to separate your story from your present-day self, you can now choose your response. Choosing to speak from your present, authentic self is empowering. Reacting from your story is disempowering. To revisit the Viktor Frankl quote, "In choosing your response is where your freedom and growth lies." I knew conquering this step would be a big area of growth for me. I also knew it wasn't going to happen overnight. I was essentially rewriting the operating system of my mind.

~

You may be thinking, "WHAT IF THE PRESENT DAY YOU ISN'T *strong? What if she is doubtful, or ashamed of where she is in life presently?"* I challenge you to dig deeper and question whether that is you or your story? You had to be strong to get to where you are now, you have overcome many obstacles, made hard choices, left toxic relationships and careers; so even though your reality might not be your ultimate desire, you get to acknowledge how strong you are inside. That version of you is in there, I promise! We just need to get her to come out more.

The plan had been created, and the next step was implementation. However, this was not something I could just do; I needed to be triggered. So, I patiently waited... and then one day it happened: a disagreement over something pointless arose between Nick and I, and I could feel myself shrinking. My awareness was heightened, and I took the next step: I stopped mid-disagreement and said out loud to myself, "Myka, thank you for trying to protect me, but I got this." Then I changed my posture, and my tone of voice, took the emotion out of the conversation, and had a logical dialog with him."

I remember him looking at me with a "what the hell just happened?" look. "Who's Myka?" he asked. "Did you just lose your mind?"

"No," I replied with a satisfied and slightly cocky smile. "I'm retraining my mind."

That night I told Nick everything I had been discovering in my Selfish Hours. The best part: it made so much sense to him. He had been silently watching my journey and letting me grow without interfering. He understood Myka and could notice me separating from that version of myself. I was obviously thankful for his support and encouragement!

The worst part: he began calling me out on it. If I would do or say something that he knew wasn't me, he would say, "Okay, Myka," in a sarcastic voice.

Of course, I would get childish, stick out my tongue to him, and try to fight, even though I knew he was right. Hey, I may have been working hard on my mindset, but I didn't like it when someone else pointed it out to me (insert image of a kid sticking her tongue out behind someone's back).

The Deepest Cut

"   I don't think of all the misery, but the beauty that still
    remains.

— Anne Frank

DURING AN EARLY MORNING SELFISH HOUR, I ASKED MY
normal question at the end of my meditation: "Selfish Hour, what do
you want to tell me today?" In my mind I heard, "The deepest cut." I
knew exactly what it meant, but I didn't feel I was ready to go there. I
also knew it was time to do just that.

My need to overachieve began to blossom when my mom and I
had the conversation in the Cadillac before my freshman game, but
the seed was planted long before that moment. That conversation
only watered it. The reason I felt this overwhelming need to overachieve, wasn't because I would be a disappointment to my family, it
was because of the brokenness in my home.

A flood of thoughts came to me that made me feel heavy,
followed by a lump in my throat and big crocodile tears. I knew I
needed to face the circumstances I had witnessed as a kid within my

family, but I tried with every ounce of my being to bury my feelings, and trick myself into thinking I was over the most hurtful part of my past. Here's the "ah-ha" moment that morning: I didn't have closure because it was the deepest cut.

When I was in fourth grade, my oldest brother got married to his high school sweetheart, and there was a shift in our family dynamic, but I was too young to understand what exactly had happened. To this day, I still do not know what happened, and after this much time, I don't believe that they even know, but my dad and my oldest brother stopped speaking. Was there a fight? Malicious words exchanged? No one knows because my family wrote the book on avoiding feelings and tough conversations.

My brother got married in March, and by Thanksgiving our family dynamic took on a different form. The aroma of turkey in the oven filled the house, the sound of a football game blared from the TV, and I played while waiting for the meal to be ready. Dinner was to be served at 4 p.m., so right before that I put on my favorite dress and sat on the couch near the front window waiting for their Honda to pull into the driveway. My mom told me she invited them, and I was filled with hope I would be seeing them soon. I remember being so excited, thinking about the family eating together in the evening, the laughter, and the hope of someone playing a game with me after.

I kept yelling to my mom in the kitchen, "Here comes a car. Oh wait, it's not them." Time passed, and I yelled again full of hope, "I know they are coming, Mom." An hour passed and I still sat eagerly awaiting their arrival. As the clock ticked, my heart sank lower and lower, hope deflating like a tire that was going flat. This memory is so clear, I can still see myself sitting there and feel the tension rise in the house. I was the age my oldest daughter is now, and as a parent you try to protect your children from sadness, but that moment was the first time I felt true sadness and heartbreak.

My mom began speaking to me, but it sounded like Charlie Brown's teacher, "Wah, Wah," as I sat by the window until darkness fell. They never showed. Thanksgiving is a day to be grateful and show appreciation to those around you, but that year no one felt grateful and we ate dinner in silence with broken hearts. It was the beginning of the end for our family.

My dad drowned the pain from his severed relationship with alcohol and rarely spoke my brother's name, while my mom cried a lot. I would come downstairs, and find her crying at the kitchen table. I would walk into her bedroom where she sat on the edge of the bed wiping away tears. Today, when I think of my brother, I think of my mom's sadness and how it made me angry for many years. Unbeknownst to me, watching her tears created a wall around my heart that was spray painted with the words, "Don't trust men. They only cause pain." Through my years of dating, I approached every relationship with an expiration date, because I would not commit and did not trust. My belief was men will only hurt you and cause you to cry.

I didn't understand my role in the new dynamics of our family. I often felt caught in the middle and was supposed to be friendly and nice with all parties. Other times I was fueled by anger that my brother could turn his back on his family. At my young age no one explained to me what happened, so I only had my imagination to rely on. It went on like this for many years. I still feel like that little eight-year-old at the window wanting my family to have love and laughter at the dinner table.

My need to overachieve wasn't fueled by trying not to disappoint my family, that was only a disguise. Hidden behind it was the need to attract all the attention to me so no one would see the dysfunction of our family. If the outside world was watching my achievements no one would see that my dad drank too much, my mom always carried tissues, my middle brother is a workaholic, and my oldest brother and his family are no longer part of our immediate family.

When I was finally able to look at my role in the family from a bird's eye view many years later, I understood it. I wanted my star to shine so bright that maybe, just maybe I would achieve something that all my family would have to come together in support, and then they would talk and become a connected family again.

I have unknowingly done an award-winning performance in my role. I was a star basketball player, a competitive clog dancer, I won beauty pageants and modeling awards, I excelled at my career and won professional awards, people paid to hear me speak, I wrote books, and even with all of these achievements, I didn't bring my family back together which is what eight-year-old me had always wanted.

For the first time, I acknowledged my eight-year-old self, loved her, and gave her permission to accept my family for who they are. My role was to just live for me and what makes my light shine bright. I cannot control my family, even though I really want to.

What I really want to say to each of them is this:

Dad, you have a disease and I accept who you are and know that you aren't going to change. I don't always like you, but I will always love you.

Todd, I wish our relationship was closer like when we were young. I know you have many feelings buried, and I hope one day we can have an open conversation.

Mom, I'm sad for you. I'm sad for what you had to deal with, I'm sad that I wasn't more understanding, I'm sad your heart is broken. I admire how strong you are; that your broken heart is slowly mending, and I know the cuts run deep for you, too. I am proud to be your daughter, because you taught me what unconditional love really means.

John, I don't know your side of the story and, at this point, does it really matter? I know the cut is deep for you, too."

Before I was able to begin healing from this deep cut, I needed to find the lesson in the dysfunction that is my family. The lesson I already knew but needed to be reinforced. I can't change the circumstance, I can only change my thoughts about it. My family has not shared a meal together, or even been in the same room in over twenty-five years. I love my family, and even though I may not agree with their choices, I know they are doing what they feel is right for them. They are each hurting in their own way, and that's their journey. I can't change anyone, or the dynamic of our family, and I released myself from that self-prescribed pressure. I blessed myself with the freedom to let go of trying to mend the relationships. I just allowed it to be what it is. Coincidently, once I released the need for things to be how I want them to be, there have been steps of reconciliation that even I was surprised about.

Life gets put into perspective when someone leaves this world or health issues arise that open your eyes to the inevitable fact that life is short and goes by faster as you get older. Living with resentment, anger, and bitterness doesn't hurt the other person, it only hurts you.

I hope this chapter has made you think of that one person or more that you need to bless and release. I highly encourage you to do so, because holding onto negative feelings and not forgiving does nothing but ultimately hurt and weigh you down. All you are doing is drinking poison and hoping the other person feels the pain. It's bad for your health and will show up in physical forms in your body.

When you bless and release, what you are essentially doing is forgiving. Forgiveness doesn't mean you are condoning or accepting the action of another, nor that you are giving up on your perspective or truth. You are purely releasing yourself from the negative control that person or those events have upon your life, and taking one hundred percent control of your response to what has happened.

The F-Word

> The weak can never forgive. Forgiveness is the attribute of the strong.
>
> — Mahatma Gandhi

FORGIVENESS IS A WORD THAT FELT DISTANT TO ME FOR MANY years. It's easy to forgive small things like a petty fight with your spouse, or when a friend shows up thirty minutes late to a lunch date. That is easy to get over. The forgiveness I'm talking about is the deep-seated pain that we buried so long ago we almost forget that it is there. We have hidden it so well in our psyche that until we get silent and look inward, we don't even acknowledge that it's there. Avoiding is so much easier than facing, dealing, and acknowledging.

I didn't realize the deep pain and resentment I had buried for my family until my Selfish Hours. I didn't want to think about it, let alone *feel* the immense feelings associated with it. There are lessons we are supposed to learn from our family, whether it's how to do or how not to do something. Our family is meant to prepare us to help other people and fulfill our purpose during our time on this earth.

The hard part is acknowledging it and taking the time to learn the lessons. I found comfort in hiding my feelings and pretending like nothing was wrong. However, this is also one of the reasons I drank. I drank not only to push Myka away, but also to bury my feelings of pain toward my family. Facing these feelings without the influence of alcohol was what made this process hard, but I knew it was the only way to do it.

Growing up in a house with a parent who is an alcoholic, watching it only get worse, and oddly accepting it while giving him an out by saying, "It's just dad. He's been drinking," plays tricks with your mind. It wasn't until I became older and worked on my emotional and mental wellness, that I was able to see the years of pain in his eyes, instead of seeing a man with no control. Alcoholism is a self-inflicted disease, because you can't become an alcoholic without first picking up the drink and swallowing it.

Alcohol is a comfort and a reliable friend, and my dad grew accustomed to using it to function through his day. My mom and dad went to the funeral of one of his closest cousins. They had been close since they were young children. My mom told me that my dad kept saying, "Let's go. I'm ready to go," while my mom was talking to family members that she hadn't seen in a long time. She was frustrated, and called me later telling me how annoying Dad was. She told me he didn't say much on the hour drive home, but as soon as they got home, he poured a big glass of wine then felt ready to chat. It made me realize that my dad was hurting, but without having alcohol at the funeral, he didn't like feeling the feelings that were surfacing inside of him. He needed to get out of there and pour something into his body to escape the feelings.

Alcohol takes his physical, mental, and emotional pain away. I am not condoning his choice, but I was finally able to see why he chose it. It helped him to forget his real-life struggles and slip away into another place. I know he loves my mom, me, and my kids, but he doesn't have a relationship with his first-born son and his family, and he has watched his wife of more than fifty years suffer because of it.

When you hold onto such sadness, guilt, and anger in your heart, forgetting seems to be the only solution there is.

Forgiving my dad had nothing to do with him; it had to with me and my expectation of what a father was supposed to be. When I watched Nick father our daughters, I created an image in my head of what a dad is "supposed" to be, and when my dad didn't fill that specific role, I got mad and resentful. Accepting what is, and who he is, allowed me to look at myself and the expectation I placed on him, which opened a space for me to bless and release. I still get annoyed, frustrated, and feel angry inside, but in those moments I check myself and realize that it has nothing to do with me. He is sick, and he is choosing to stay sick because it's easier than the alternative. He is choosing to escape rather than face feelings, have uncomfortable conversations, and learn how not to be the victim.

My girls and I wanted to surprise my parents by arriving a day early for our planned vacation to visit them, so we loaded up the SUV and drove six hours on a hot Friday in July. When we pulled in the driveway at around 2 p.m., I watched my dad stumble into our back garage without noticing us. At that moment, I thought about how he had aged and how frail he looked. Within minutes of seeing him, I knew he was drunk. My heart ached, and I felt disappointed and angry that my kids had to witness him, even though at their young age and not seeing him often, they probably didn't realize. I later learned that he had been at church drinking wine with the priest. At one point in my life, I would have found it comical, but that time I didn't.

The next morning, I overheard my parents chatting and my mom asking my dad if he was going to church on Sunday.

My dad's response was the turning point for my forgiveness. He said in a beaten down voice, "I'm not going to church. Did you see what the priest did to me yesterday?"

I had to fight off every urge in my body not to step in and scream, "You are a grown ass man who chose to drink the wine. He didn't pour it down your throat." All of my mindset tools guided me to turn around, go to my room, and sit in silence with my thoughts. *He thinks he is a victim.* It was at that moment I realized how sick he was. It wasn't slurred words, or the forgetfulness from drinking, it was the core belief that everyone was out to get him. I learned from ACOA that when you start drinking and become addicted, you stop developing emotionally. My father is stuck at fifteen years-old in his emotional development. My anger turned to sadness. I wanted to view my dad as a superhero, as someone that is strong as an ox. However, my expectations are not reality, so I forgave. I released the noose from around my heart that had been squeezing tight for years. In the silence that day, I found the strength and acceptance to see what is.

Forgiveness is merely letting go of your negative feelings or thoughts of revenge, frustration, bitterness, and judgment toward the person who hurt you. Forgiving someone has nothing to do with the other person and everything to do with you.

Being Aware of Being Aware

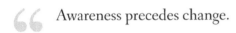 Awareness precedes change.

— Robin Sharma

KNOWING WHAT YOU KNOW NOW, WHAT WOULD YOU SAY TO your twenty-year-old self? When I hear this question and look back at my life, it causes me to smile at the good memories, and cringe at some I wish I didn't remember. If I could give my younger self advice, it would be to become self-aware sooner.

Awareness to being present has made the biggest impact on my personal growth. Self-awareness guided me to recognize Myka's role in my life, and it has taught me to make decisions that are in alignment with my values and authentic self, instead of being influenced by how others will perceive me. I feel I would have come into my own sooner if I had just been aware. We are all on a journey with a long road to travel, but having awareness will help you not to wander too far from the path. Instead of looking at the world from the lens of *why me?* look at it as *what lesson is this supposed to teach me?*

If there are things about yourself that you want to change, self-awareness is where you start. If there are things about other people you want to change, self-awareness is where you start. Now that may sound a bit off, but let me explain. We can waste a lot of time and energy trying to change someone else, but we are not able to change other people no matter how hard we try, and if they do change, it's not for the right reasons and it will only backfire at some point.

I watched this with my mother always (in her words) "getting on my dad's case" about his drinking. She would take a beer away from him, give him an evil look when she heard the can open, and then the next morning when he was sober have a one-sided conversation with him about his drinking. She would talk, he would tolerate, and then leave the room. This pattern has been playing on repeat for more than fifty years and nothing has changed. He hasn't changed and she hasn't changed. Think in your own life where you have a pattern of wanting and complaining about something to change, but that is all it is: a pattern of anger, words, and resentment repeated. Bring awareness into the picture and you will understand you can't change the other person, but you can change who you are in relation to that person.

You may choose to physically reduce the amount of time you spend with them or accept who they are and let them be them. Stop trying to change them and change yourself.

When you begin to feel an old pattern surfacing, or something triggering you, tune in to the thought and become aware of the feeling that comes with that thought. Watching *Jeopardy* with Nick is a major trigger for me. I instantly feel stupid because I can barely finish reading the question before he belts out the answer. Now I choose not to put the show on. The power of awareness activates the moment you consciously choose to assign a different meaning to what's happening. The way we react to people or situations is based on past conditioning. Even if the experience is the same, your response can be different. Just because you reacted a certain way a week ago, a day ago, or an hour ago you hold the power to choose how you want to respond the next time.

During my Selfish Hours, I was finally able to take an honest look at my life, and I saw all the moments where I thought I was a victim, but it was only because that was the meaning I assigned to it. We often forget, or don't even know that we own the pen to script our story. *We* decide how we want it to go. Too often we hand the pen over to other people—social media, friends, spouses, or family members. We do this for likes, comments, people to like us... to people please. The question is: at what expense do you choose to hand over your pen? The answer: your true self, your authenticity. All this does is leave you feeling empty and out of alignment with who you really are. When someone says, "I lost myself," it usually comes from this exact scenario. Trying to make everyone else happy completely displaces what brings you joy, and makes you feel complete.

I often hear clients say, "I'm happy when my kids are happy." Making your happiness dependent upon other people will never truly fulfill you. Also, what is that teaching your kids? Look to others for happiness. Here's a truth: true joy, happiness, and fulfillment is found through looking internally—never externally.

I will often get asked, "How do I look inside?" The answer: you have to get quiet. You have to want to get quiet, to sort through the clutter in your mind, to listen to what's really going on. You may notice the voices in your head sound like a crazy person. You will notice you have many, if not countless stories swirling around when you get silent. Write them down. When you bring them to life by writing it on paper, you will see what you are truly processing. Learn how to have a conversation with yourself. Not the conversation you have while in the shower, driving, or cooking dinner but a different type of conversation.

If someone stole my laptop and read some of the things I have typed, they would be getting me help! I ask myself, *Why do you feel this way?* and I answer, *I feel this way because that person should not talk that way to me,* and I keep the conversation going. My fingers will keep typing freely until I am either crying or laughing at how ridiculous it all sounds. But it leads to clarity and gives answers to *why.*

Self-awareness is a deep understanding of you: your values, thoughts, and emotions. Learn to pay attention to your thoughts, or who or what influenced them.

Self-awareness is the first step in taking control of your life. Here are a few tips to help build your awareness muscle:

- Sit in a quiet and distraction free space. Close your eyes, breathe in for a count of four, and breath out for a count of four. Do this a few times until your mind starts to calm and your internal noise gets quiet.
- Get a notepad and journal.
- Ask these questions: What truly makes me happy? What activities do I love?
- Then ask the question *why?*
- What activity do I not do anymore?
- What is something I do and really dislike?
- What is something I have always wanted to try but never did?
- Create your own Selfish Hour each morning. Set boundaries like no email and no social media. Just you, your mind, a pen, and a piece of paper.
- Pay attention to your thoughts, words, emotions, and feelings.
- What stories are you telling yourself that are leading to your emotions?
- What emotions are driving your actions?
- Are they your feelings or are you doing something to make someone else happy?

- Does it really make you mad or has it always made you mad and it has become a conditioned response?
- Do you respond "I don't care" when you really do?

This is not easy, but it will be the BEST thing you can ever do for yourself. Get to know and understand you!

Decision Making

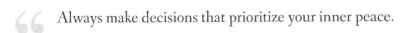
Always make decisions that prioritize your inner peace.

— Anonymous

HAVE YOU EVER BEEN FACED WITH A DIFFICULT DECISION, AND your gut feeling was telling you one thing, but your mind was telling you the complete opposite, and you only listened to your mind later to say, *I knew in my gut I shouldn't do it, but I did it anyway?* That is self-awareness. Listen to your gut feelings because that is your soul speaking to you. This is the place from where you can choose to live in alignment with the best version of yourself.

This is a technique that I learned and use often to make tough decisions. I have been practicing it for years and don't even know who to credit it to. I am going to assume it was one of the many voices I heard through my earbuds in meditation in a Selfish Hour. This will help quiet the mind so you can truly listen to your gut/inner voice/soul—whatever you choose to call it.

Before we begin, I want you to think of a decision you need to make. It can be something small like, *What do I want for dinner tonight?* or something major like, *Should I quit my job?* Assign Option A and Option B.

- Option A is doing something.
- Option B is not doing something.

Examples:

- Option A: I get Chinese food for dinner.
- Option B: I get pizza for dinner.

- Option A: I quit my job.
- Option B: I stick with my current job and give it my all.

Sit quietly with no distractions, close your eyes, and get still for a few moments. This is the hardest part. Stop thinking about needing to pay a bill, the person you forgot to call back, or whether your child did their homework. Try your best to take five minutes for yourself and forget about all that stuff; I promise it will still be there when you are done with this exercise.

Start with all your focus on Option A. Picture yourself enjoying Chinese food, chicken lo mein, wonton soup, dumplings, and cracking the fortune cookie at the end of the meal. How do you feel after consuming the food and cleaning up? Really feel and sense yourself eating it for dinner.

Or if it's quitting your job, think about the conversation with your boss, writing and giving your resignation letter, packing up your desk, and driving away. Visualize everything, even waking up the next morning and moving onto the new venture. How do you feel? Who do you call first? What do you say? Really feel that you quit your job.

After imagining that for a few moments, open your eyes and bring awareness to how your body feels. What emotions are going through you? Are you feeling light and airy, or are you feeling heavy? Did your body temperature rise and you feel hot, or do you feel comfortable and at ease? Do you feel anxious or excited? Grab a pen and paper and write down your feelings. Don't listen to the voices in your head, only pay attention to your feelings. Your thoughts are attached to your ego and feelings are more attached to your alignment/inner source.

Now do the same thing with Option B. Fully immerse yourself in getting pizza or not quitting your job. How do you feel? Visualize every step and commit in your mind to it. Nine times out of ten, you will feel the exact opposite to how you felt with Option A.

Your answer is very clear. What *feels* right for you is the answer. Now it's your choice to follow it.

I did this exact exercise based on a trip I was supposed to take. Option A was going on the trip, and Option B was not going on the trip. When I visualized Option A, my body got hot, I had anxiety, and I felt extremely heavy. When I closed my eyes and visualized Option B, not going on the trip, I felt light, almost as if I was floating in the room. I was smiling when I opened my eyes. I felt warm and comfortable.

However, my ego said, "Megan, you need to go on this trip. You are already committed, and you can't back out of it now. What will people think of you?"

So, what did I do? I went on the trip. The night before I left, I was up all night with anxiety. When I arrived at the destination, I knew from the moment I walked through the door I wasn't supposed to be there, and I went to the bathroom and cried. The trip and its purpose were not in alignment with who I am, and who I'm meant to be. I committed to it and still participated, but I wasn't meant to be there even though I didn't listen to my gut.

What is Possible?

ONE DAY, I WAS DRIVING AND MY FIVE-YEAR-OLD DAUGHTER Devney asked from the back seat, "Mom, what is possible?"

"What do you mean?" I replied.

"I heard you tell someone the other day that anything is possible, what does that mean?"

When they say your kids are always listening it is true, to the good stuff and the bad stuff. (She also told me one day what I say the most is, "Oh, shit!")

I love when a teaching moment for my daughters presents itself. I went on to explain that if you set your mind to something, and work hard even when it's not fun, that anything is possible.

I know my girls well enough to know exactly what she would say next. "I don't like to do things that aren't fun."

I tried to put it in terms she would understand. "You like having a clean playroom so you can find any toy you want to play with, right?"

"Yes, I love playing with my dolls, and stuffies (what she calls her stuffed animals)," she said.

"Is cleaning the playroom fun?" I asked.

"No, you and daddy always yell at us and want to throw away our toys."

I smirked. "Well, yes, that is true, because it takes you two to four hours to do a twenty-minute cleaning job. But when the playroom is cleaned, you two love it and we all do the clean room dance, right?"

"Oh, yeah, I love that part!" she said with a smile.

"See, anything is possible if you do the not fun stuff to get toward the goal."

The next morning during my Selfish Hour, I spent more time thinking about what is possible. So many of my clients want the end result: they want to be rich, they want the title, they want the top rank in their company, or to win the national championship. But, when it comes to the work, the excuses begin. Most people fall in love with the idea of the end result but that is not what you need to love; you need to fall in love with the process. If you don't love the process, you will quit along the way.

I heard a CD of Zig Ziglar talking at an Amway convention and he said something that has always stuck with me. He said, "When you get on stage and people are cheering for you, and in your bank account you have amassed tons of money, and you hit the rank or title you have worked toward, none of that really matters—it's only a moment in time. What really matters is, at the end of the day, when you look in the mirror and see who you have become in the process of attaining that goal. That is what it's all about."

What I came to understand is that it's not the goal I was seeking, it's the growth I needed to go through in order to achieve the goal. I know many people that create vision boards or write down their goals, but when it's time to do the work, their negative stories run the show and they collapse. Negative stories are the baseline for excuses, and their main purpose is to make us feel better about not wanting to do the hard work. I encounter people each day with the same exact scenario: working full time, kids at home, husband working so it falls all on mom's shoulders, and when it's time for them to do something for themselves, such as workout or work on a business, they have a long list of excuses as to why they can't do it. But, I see a smaller percentage of the same group of people that transform those excuses into fuel to achieve their goals.

Instead of using their circumstances as excuses, they use them as the motivation to work or as the catalyst to change their circumstance. They say, "I stay up after the kids go to bed to grow my business so one day I can walk away from my full time job and have financial and time freedom in my life." Everyone has the same opportunities and the same excuses, but a few people choose to be bigger than their excuses and we call them lucky when they succeed.

Right before the pandemic started, Nick bought me a Peloton bike for my fortieth birthday. One of my big goals is to be in the best shape of my life in my forties. My goal is to be healthy and feel confident wearing skinny jeans, leggings, tight tops, or a swimsuit. I have zero excuse not to work out each day because half of my office has been transformed into a gym with the Peloton bike, yoga mats, and weights.

One day, I wasn't feeling it and Nick asked as a supportive husband, "What workout did you do today?"

I told him I wasn't feeling it and was going to skip that day.

He looked at me and went into coaching mode and said one sentence with conviction. "You need to be bigger than your biggest excuse."

Damnit. I hate when he is right, and he was right. We all want the results but sometimes not the process to get the results.

When you have a big dream and begin working toward it, it will introduce you to a part of yourself you don't know right now. You need to fall in love with the process. The messiness, the failures, the pain of doing it when you don't want to, the uncomfortableness, and the sacrifice that comes with it. The next time you don't want to work out, stay up late to work on your business, or do the work to get your master's degree, you need to reconnect with your deeper purpose for doing it. What is driving you to achieve your big desire? If the driving force is external gratification, you will fall victim to your excuses.

Think about your motivations. Do you want to lose weight to impress someone, or do you want to become healthy so you can do more with your life? Do you want to hit the top rank of your company so you can have more money and get your family out of debt? Yes, that is a great motivator, but it is still external. Once you have the money and the debt is wiped out, will that make you a happier or better person? External goals achieved cannot fill internal voids untouched.

I had a "ah-ha" moment during this Selfish Hour, the whole process of writing this book I had said to myself and others, "I don't identify as a writer. I am a speaker," and I created an excuse as to why it's hard for me to write this book. Yes, this is Myka showing her face again in those moments. See, even when you do this work, it can still get you when you least expect it. I want the end result of being a bestselling author, but I have not fallen in love with the process of writing every day, I have only flirted with it. That's the dirty work. I give myself the excuse of not feeling inspired, saying that I can only write when I am. All I did was create a great story about myself, the beauty of identifying our stories is that we can rewrite them. Once you rewrite a story about yourself, you shift your thoughts, energy, and execution around the activity.

This all started with my five-year-old asking me what is possible. When you create awareness around your own bullshit stories, and you can rewrite them into positive stories that eliminate excuses and push you forward...anything *is* possible.

It Wasn't About the Spider

> Seeing a spider isn't the biggest problem, it becomes a problem when it disappears.
>
> — Anonymous

WHILE I WAS SOUND ASLEEP ONE NIGHT, NICK WAKES ME UP and says, "Are you awake?"

I immediately jumped up and said, "What's wrong? Are you okay?" Before he could speak, every worst possible answer ran through my mind in less than three seconds: cancer, having a heart attack, a murderer is breaking into the house, you gambled away our life savings.

His response was not at all what I expected. He simply said, "I can't shut my mind off."

Oh, welcome to the club—I fully understand this! We went into a three-hour conversation about everything: pandemic, careers, possibility of losing a job due to the economy, what ifs, our life's purpose, and feeling out of control on the things you normally have control over. Our relationship has strengthened over the years, and since opening up with him about my internal struggles, it made this conversation have so much depth. Having a relationship where you don't feel judged and can speak freely is something I thank God for every day, because I know a lot of people don't have this.

The uncertainty of the pandemic, and not knowing when it would end or the repercussions it would bring is a thing, I know many of us spent hours thinking about. Nick couldn't shut his mind off. He wasn't able to sleep at night, and that affected his mood during the day, his concentration dipped, and that only perpetuated more scarcity thoughts. He was caught in a vicious cycle he didn't know how to break.

After listening to him, I went into coaching mode and he listened and received my suggestions. We are a team, and I took pride once again in being the rock at this time in our marriage. We fell asleep in the early hours of the morning holding hands. The next morning, we went about our days not mentioning anything from the night before because all of the words had been spoken.

But the more I replayed the conversation in my head, the more my anxiety grew. I had taken on his worries and his concerns and was sporting them like I was walking down the runway. The empath in me was in full swing and I felt the weight of it holding me down. Knowing he was in a fragile place, I didn't want to put anything on him, so I held it in. I meditated on it; I took it out on the Peloton, but, after weeks, the worry consumed me. I was losing sleep worried about him. I felt sorry for us, I felt sorry for him, I felt sorry for the state of our world. I had all the tools and resources at my fingertips to clear my mind and release this worry, but it wasn't working.

One night, Nick was packing to leave on his annual deer hunting trip in Wisconsin. I grew up in the country with a family of hunters, but I still don't get sitting in the cold for hours waiting for a deer to walk by just so you can fire a shot. While he packed his warmest clothes, I sat on the bed chatting with him.

All of a sudden, I looked over and saw a small spider making its way near the bed. I jumped up and ran into the bathroom to get a tissue to dispose of this arachnid. When I walked out of the bathroom, Nick had used his hand to shoo the spider away from the bed toward the wall. In that moment, all of the pent-up worry, anxiety, frustrations, fears, you name it, they all came rushing to the surface.

I screamed, "What the fuck did you do!? There is now a spider in our room, and I can't find it. What are you thinking?" And I couldn't let it go. I screamed a primal scream that came from the depth of my soul. Our five-year-old daughter walked into the bedroom while I was screaming, swearing, and basically losing my shit. Typically, we do not argue in front of our children, so she looked at me and started laughing because the visual must have looked ridiculous. However, I was in such a release space that when I saw her staring at me, I wasn't even phased.

Nick asked if he should call the psych ward and said repeatedly, "Why are you going so crazy? You are nuts."

The whole scene lasted for about three minutes and then I went to talk to our daughters to apologize for my behavior, but they didn't care about mama looking crazy, they cared more about the spider coming into their room. I explained to them that just like they sometimes throw tantrums or cry and scream when they don't get their way, that was what just happened to mommy. I'm not perfect. I'm still growing and learning too.

As I sat in silence the next morning during my Selfish Hour, I had time to process my crazy episode, and then it became crystal clear for me: it had nothing to do with the spider. It had to do with me holding in all my worry, trying to take on more responsibility with the kids and house so Nick didn't have to do it, and I felt anxious that he was leaving for eleven days and I had to play the role of mom and dad while he got to step away from responsibility and sit in the woods.

I was jealous and mad at him and mad at myself for knowing how to handle my emotions but not choosing to do so. These feelings were placed on top of the stress of 2020, the approaching holidays, and virtual schooling. In that moment the previous evening, I reacted and released. It wasn't pretty, but I felt damn good afterward. The lesson to learn here is even when you think you are being strong and putting everything on your plate to help out someone you love, if you don't take care of yourself and express yourself, a little arachnid may cause you to lose your shit.

The Antidote to Overwhelm

> Deep breathing is our nervous system's love language.
>
> — Dr. Lauren Fogel Mersy

PRACTICING GRACE BECAME A REGULAR OCCURRENCE FOR ME throughout this journey. When Myka, or one of my stories would get the best of me and I consciously or unconsciously knew what I was doing, I would get pissed at myself. *Come on Megan, you should know better.* I work on my mindset daily, and I know I have negative stories that are going to come up, but why does this keep happening. Will I ever grow past this?

Unfortunately, "no" is what I learned. Negative thoughts are always going to creep in, managing your mind is a continual practice with no true end. As humans we are designed to learn, grow, and evolve, so at each new chapter of life, and with the new experiences that come with them, more stories will present themselves. But there are typically one or two core stories that we always come back to. For me it was, *I'm not smart enough.* When I deal with other negative thoughts, I peel back the onion, and nine times out of ten the issue has to do with my eleven-year-old self not feeling smart enough. This is where the practice of *grace* needs to come into play. Giving yourself grace is about being kind to yourself. I practice being kind to my present and future self because I have been mean to my past self.

Creating a breathing practice has been a helpful tool that I have also taught my daughters how to use. When the feeling of overwhelm creeps in—you know those days when it seems like everything you touch creates more work for you and you need to be somewhere fifteen minutes ago—the thought of giving yourself grace feels like the last possible option because you don't even have time for that. You need to get shit done. I have learned my tendencies well enough to know when it's time for a breathing technique. I stop whatever I'm doing, close my eyes, and breathe in through my nose for a count of four, hold for a count of four, and let it out through my mouth to a count of four. I do this a few times until I feel my energy shift. Then I focus on five things I am grateful for. This has a way of centering me and bringing me back to the present moment. Most times the things you are worrying about or that are making you a little cray-cray are self-induced. Yes, your plate is full, but focus on one task at a time, since that is all you can do. The question to ask yourself after your gratitude statement is, "What is the next best thing I can do?" And then do it.

The four in-four out breathing practice comes in handy with my daughter when she gets herself worked up. Before a test, a soccer game, or when we are running late for the bus, she gets flustered and the tears begin to well up in the corners of her eyes.

I say to her, 'Four in, four out," and she knows to stop, take a few deep breaths, exhale and reset herself.

When I learned that overwhelm is just a thought that I can change, I had to sit with that for a while. I used to think that being "busy" or feeling overwhelmed was a badge of honor. That meant I was important and had a lot going on. But I realized that it actually means there is no plan. Everyone has lots going on, yes some more than others, but a very natural response to "How are things?" is typically "Good, just really busy." People love to feel busy because it makes them needed and important. I love to do word swaps, and my favorite swap is the saying "abundant" instead of "busy." Busy sounds chaotic and out of control, while abundant sounds blessed and plentiful. Feel the difference from above. "How are things?" "Good, my schedule is very abundant." It makes you feel grateful for a full plate instead of seeing it as a burden.

The feeling of overwhelm leads to procrastination, and either nothing gets done or it gets done poorly. The antidote to overwhelm is a plan. We often know all of the things we need to do but fail to organize it in a way that releases the overwhelm so we can move into productive action.

To create a plan of action, I start by doing a brain dump and getting everything that I need to do out of my brain onto paper. Decluttering your mind is a very therapeutic process. The list of to-dos can be pick up dry cleaning, schedule doctor appointments, edit book, create hour long presentation, do three coaching sessions, prep for coaching sessions, go grocery shopping, pack for trip, pick up gift for kids' birthday party, etc.

Once that is done, I prioritize the list in order of importance from the activities that need my attention first or which have the earliest deadline. I delegate the tasks that I don't need to do and someone else is fully capable of doing. This instantly brings a sense of calm and some actionable next steps.

I then grab my paper agenda book, as I'm old school and still find satisfaction in holding my pen and checking something off my list. I add the list of activities to my agenda, and give each a specific time when I will work on the activity and how long it will take to complete it. Most people ask me, "How do you know how long something will take to complete?" My answer is simple: "You create the timeframe." If you give yourself two hours to create a presentation, it will take you two hours. If you give yourself one hour, it will take you one hour." You know how long you need to complete an activity. However, the biggest mistake people make when adding their actions into their agenda is they schedule everything back to back with no down time or space. I rarely schedule meetings, trainings, or coaching sessions back to back, because I know the value of stepping away from my computer or having space if issues arise that need my attention.

Another tip is to write the desired outcome into the time slot. Instead of writing "work on business" or "edit book" tell yourself exactly the production that will be done in the time frame. "Follow up with the people I met at the networking event last night" or "Edit chapters 12 and 13." You look at your agenda and at 3 p.m. on Tuesday it reads, "Invite ten people to an event on Friday," and you have one hour to do it. This takes out the guesswork; you already know what you need to do. But here is the biggest issue you will face: you don't *feel* like doing what it says at that time.

Doing the brain dump and transferring it over to an agenda book is the easy part. Following through and executing on what is in the agenda is where most people struggle.

When it's time to invite people, or edit the book your mind creates every excuse as to why you don't *feel* like doing it.

- I'm tired, I didn't get much sleep last night.
- I can't focus right now.
- The argument you had with someone is the only thing going through your mind.
- No one is going to know if I don't do it.
- I will do double the work tomorrow.

This is where most people fail. Your negative thoughts win. You avoid what's on your agenda to move toward your goals and you will do something that gives you momentary pleasure to make yourself feel better. Such as snack, do laundry, clean the house, exercise, or watch Netflix. The mind is so powerful that it will trick you to believe that avoiding your agenda is the right thing to do, but then when you lay in bed at night you beat yourself up for no doing what you were excited about doing when you created your agenda. The hardest part about breaking this habit is it's typically unconscious; meaning you don't even realize you are avoiding until much later. To break this cycle is to become aware of your thoughts and feelings in the present moment. Start to pay attention to what you are doing and why you are doing it. If you are not executing what it is in your agenda, ask yourself some simple questions:

- "What is the dominant thought going through my mind right now?"
- "How am I feeling about doing what's on my agenda?"

Do your best to answer these questions without "I don't know" as an answer. I don't know is not an answer, it's an excuse. Through this practice, I have created an awareness of how I am feeling in the moment, and then I can work it backward to understand the thoughts leading me too feeling a certain way. To move forward, you need to be bigger than your biggest excuse. People that succeed, people who win the awards, people who others think are "lucky" are only those who were bigger than their biggest excuse.

Give Me a Moment
While I Overreact

❝ Life is ten percent what happens to you and ninety percent how you respond to it.

— Lou Holtz

ONE OF THE MOST IMPORTANT THINGS I LEARNED ON THIS journey is how powerful our thoughts are. Our thoughts are the epicenter of our lives, they control how we feel, how we act, and, ultimately, our results in life. Most of the time, we view the world through a pair of glasses we put on as kids. Psychologists believe that by the age of seven, most of our beliefs and habits are already formed. The glasses are clouded with beliefs from our parents and other adults in life, environmental factors, or straight up stories we created in our younger years that we played on repeat until they became a belief. When we look at people and circumstances through these lenses, we react a certain way. Learning how to respond versus reacting was a total game changer. When Nick and I had our argument that sparked this whole journey, I was a professional reactor. I knew my comfort zone reaction and easily went there.

It wasn't until I started to pay attention to my thoughts that I learned I can choose my response and not simply react. The Detachment Method was the starting point for this, because it all begins with awareness, and that leads to responding. I wanted to break down the difference between responding and reacting because most of us are professional reactors and damn good at it.

Have you ever said something without thinking? When you say something without thinking, that is your unconscious mind running the show, or your version of Myka. The scared/mad/unloved kid just jumped in the car, shoved you to the backseat, and pushed the gas to the floor in the driver seat. That is a reaction.

A reaction is based in the past and in fear. A response comes more slowly. A response weighs out the long-term effects and stays in line with your true authentic self.

When you can begin to recognize your thoughts for what they are —a hurt child, a rebel, a parent's voice, anger—then you learn to separate yourself and authentically choose a response that is in alignment with who you really are. That is when you begin to live.

Most of us don't recognize our thoughts because we have so many zooming through our minds, but we recognize how we feel. The reason we feel anxious, or fearful of something is because our thoughts led us there. I spent the greater part of my life with anxiety, and the way I released myself from those sour stomach feelings and pacing around was to shift my thoughts. My negative thoughts were the precursor to anxiety, I just never connected the dots before. In the quiet moments of my Selfish Hours is where I learned that, if my thoughts can give me anxiety, they can also take it away. I can shift my thoughts to be positive.

I constantly work on reprogramming my brain and allowing myself to release the fear of the unknown that is causing my anxiety. That is how I truly learned to separate from Myka and free myself from my past. It was all in my thoughts. We are all great fictional authors; it's all just stories we create. If we can script a negative meaning to a circumstance, we can always script a positive and empowering meaning to it. It's simply a choice. You are powerful beyond what you can imagine.

If you are in a storm right now, if life has been shitting on you, you have the power to change the story. Write a different one starting right now. You hold the pen to script the rest of your story. Don't look back and say "I should have," look forward and say "I will, because this is who I am." Step into, and be the true self you identified earlier. If you don't believe that for yourself, live in the belief I have for you, because I know that if you have read this far into this book, you want more, you know you deserve more, and I have given you the tools to make it happen. I believe in you and the recipe is simple, not easy, but simple: change your thoughts, change your story, and change your life.

Wear It

> Being different isn't a bad thing. It means you're brave
> enough to be yourself.

— Luna Lovegood from *Harry Potter*

It has become a common theme that I see with many
clients, especially women, that they give too much weight to what
other people think about them. We allow opinions of others to sway
our decision making, which in the end has us not truly living in alignment with our authentic self. It happens so often, that once we are in
adulthood we don't even know who our authentic self is because it's
buried under years of other people's opinions and influence over us.

One Saturday afternoon as a family we were going to attend a
basketball game at the university where Nick works. I told Codi, who
was five-years-old at the time, to go change either her shirt or her
pants, because she couldn't go to the game wearing her mismatched
outfit. She had on LuLaRoe leggings that were full of bright colors
moving in different directions, and her shirt was decorated with

pastel colors going in the opposite direction to the pants. She had a lot going on.

After about ten minutes, she hadn't come out of her room, so I went to check on her. I found her sitting on her bed with her knees pulled into her chest and her arms wrapped tightly around them. I could see big crocodile tears streaming down her face. She looked so cute and innocent. I sat next to her and asked what was wrong.

Through her tears she said, "Mommy, I like what I'm wearing. It feels good on. Why do I have to change?"

At that moment it felt like I had been punched in the gut. I said, "Codi, I'm sorry. If you are comfortable and feel good you don't have to change."

She wrapped her arms around me and cried even more. After hearing our conversation, Nick walked into the room at that moment with a big smile and head nod, confirming I did the right thing.

Here is what I realized in that gut punch moment. I wanted her clothes to match so people wouldn't judge *me* as a mom. I was squashing my daughter's individuality in the name of caring what people will think of me.

She went on that afternoon to be authentically herself in her mismatched color swirling outfit. She was happy, polite, a great friend, and a fantastic big sister. She wore a beautiful smile on her face that would have been missing had she changed her clothes.

Think about how often we do this and don't even realize. We have become a society that cares so much about the perfect Instagram photo and making our life look like we have it all together for other people's approval. The only approval we ever need is our own and God's, and He loves us no matter what.

Codi taught me a powerful lesson that day that forever shifted my perspective. She taught me that I needed to look at myself and not give my insecurities to her.

When we brought Codi home from the hospital for the first time, Nick said something that I will never forget as we looked at this little human that was now our responsibility. He said, "Our job is to keep her alive and make sure she is not an asshole."

A lot of assholes dress really nice. Codi is happy, has good manners, is a well-liked kid by her friends, teachers, and other parents. She embraces her individuality and I have learned to embrace it as well. The rule in our house that was created that day: as long as it's weather appropriate, wear it!

Where are you hiding your individuality to win people's approval? Is it in how you dress, how you present yourself at work, or with a certain crowd of friends, or around your family or in-laws? Do you take care of everyone else at the expense of your own authenticity? I feel on some level most people go through this trying to fit in at some stage of life. However, what is the cost of hiding your individuality? Who benefits? It's clearly not you—it's whoever you are trying to please. Do they really benefit by missing out on your truest self?

Continually showing up as someone else to make others happy is a feeding ground for resentment. You may feel good at first, when the waters are calm and everyone is happy, but after a while, you begin to resent the people you are trying to please because it cost you... yourself. If other people don't like you, that is their negative story, not yours. Don't take their story and make it yours.

Why Hustling is Not Enough

> Only when your intent and action are in alignment can you create the reality you desire.

— Steve Maraboli

I BECAME A CORPORATE REFUGEE IN NOVEMBER 2017. THE DAY I quit my job, I felt unbelievably calm. I had visualized that moment in my head so many times it was already done, and the physical act of doing it was effortless. I drove home free from the chains that had bound me for so many years. Knowing I had a family to support and house to run meant it was game time for me to build my coaching business. I had been building a business while working my full-time job and already had some clients, but I needed to concentrate on marketing, social media, and networking to really build a business I was proud of. I embraced the challenge and the unknown. It was a challenge that most people would never take on, but I was ready to tackle it like a WWF wrestler.

Each year, I pick a word to be my mantra that guides me. In 2018, my word was hustle. Growing up an athlete, married to a coach, this word was etched into my brain. I knew it's what I needed to do to grow, reach more people with my services, and create the life that was on the vision board in my office. I loved this word so much I found fake tattoos of a cursive *Hustle* and wore it on my wrist to remind me daily of what I needed to do.

Each morning after my Selfish Hour and getting the family out the door, I went to my desk and hustled. For six months, I was grinding each day and had made little progress. Month after month, I knew what I needed to make to cover my expenses, and each month I fell short. I was making money, but not enough. I had clients, but not enough. I posted on social media, but not enough. I went to networking events, but not enough. I spent quality time with Nick and our girls, but it wasn't enough. I needed to hustle more, I needed to do more, because no matter how much I did, it wasn't enough.

Each day, no matter how much I hustled, *I* wasn't enough. I attached my self-worth to my results and felt that I just wasn't enough. Have you ever tried to be your best when you feel you are not enough? It's not possible. It feels fake and forced and people can see right through you, even when you think you should be winning an award for your performance. Searching outside for validation and satisfaction—that we are enough—will always be short lived because it has to come from within.

One morning at the end of my Selfish Hour meditation, I looked down and saw the script *Hustle* on my wrist. The constant hustle was what made me feel like not enough. Right then, I had a divine download. *Hustle works best when you are in alignment.* Ping... light bulb moment. I wasn't in alignment, so my hustle was like my Peloton bike, spinning like crazy but not going anywhere.

I did a quick beat-up session on myself for not having this realization sooner. One would think with all the mindset work I did I should have known, but I didn't let the pity party last long. I left my office, got some baby oil, and rubbed the *Hustle* off my wrist and out of my thoughts. I switched my word to *alignment*, changed my work routine, and energetically everything shifted for me. Before I began creating content, I did a visualization meditation to get myself grounded, then I would work. The words flowed easily, I felt much more confident asking people to be on my podcast or have me on theirs. I began showing up as the person I wanted to be, not the person I thought I had to be, which is a liberating feeling. The second half of 2018, I made five times what I made in the first half of that year. It wasn't astronomical, but it was effortless to create because I worked from alignment.

Alignment for me meant that I was getting out of my own way. I lived in faith that if I showed up to serve people, instead of looking at each prospect as a way to pay my bills and feed my family, my life and work would flow better. And it did. Giving myself permission to change my word mid-year was exactly what I needed to do, pushing through on hustle would have ultimately driven me to burnout, overwhelm, and resenting my business. Shifting my mindset from *hustle* to *alignment* was the adjustment I needed to regain the sense that I am enough.

Being in alignment with your highest and best self means you feel powerful and peaceful at the same time. It allows the channel to open so you can receive the messages God is trying to send. It means that the words flow effortlessly through my fingers onto the keyboard. I don't judge myself. I don't compare myself to others. I just create with ease. If something feels icky or gives me a bad feeling, I simply don't do it or proceed with caution. I learned how to fall in the love with the process and not the end result.

#metoo

> Things don't happen to you; they happen for you.
>
> — Tony Robbins

In October 2019, about two years after becoming a corporate refugee, I partnered with my longtime friend and mentor, Bob Heilig. We are the definition of life coming full circle. We first met in 2003 in a network marketing business, where he was my upline and the person who taught me how to dream. Prior to his mentorship, I didn't believe that if I wanted something I could actually work hard and get it.

I thought I was on the path to go to school, get a good job, work hard, get promoted, have good benefits, and work until it was time to retire with a decent pension. Bob introduced me to personal development books. Books like *Think and Grow Rich* by Napoleon Hill, *Leading an Inspired Life* by Jim Rohn, *Rich Dad, Poor Dad* by Robert Kiyosaki, and every book from John Maxwell. I became a sponge, my mind expanded, and I realized in my early twenties that I am a dreamer. If you are a dreamer, you understand what I mean: you have a fire that is ignited inside of you, and every day you have a desire to do and be more. You have this drive to do what others won't and grow whatever impossible dream is planted inside of you.

At that point in my life, my dream wasn't crystal clear. I just knew I wanted to impact people's lives in a positive way and do it so much that Oprah wanted to interview me. I thought my vehicle was going to be through network marketing, but I had so much personal growth to do that it didn't manifest until many years later.

Bob and I had always said we were going to achieve great things together. We have different parents, but I feel more connected to him as a brother than I do my own blood. We share a similar vision, similar values, and a passion for helping others. He brought me on as the first coach outside of him to coach in his online membership community. It's a leadership development program teaching network marketers how to grow a sustainable and lucrative business using our philosophy of Love, Serve, Grow. I do weekly mindset and business coaching, and as the membership grew, so did my confidence in my coaching ability. I added certified life coach to my tool-belt and kept growing myself daily.

One particular coaching session will forever weigh on my mind. The sessions are run via Zoom as open coaching, so clients can ask me anything regarding their mindset struggles, or as we refer to them Red Light Stories. Honestly, there really are only a handful of Red-Light Stories people have, but they disguise them to feel like they are the only person in the world who feels this way, or that it has ever happened to. It's usually some flavor of "I'm not good enough," or "I'm not worthy." My coaching skills are very sharp with helping people shift their stories to one that will empower them to take positive action. But on this particular day, it was God's will that the first woman who shared took the conversation in a completely different direction and caught me on my heels.

Her life circumstance was that she had been sexually molested as a child, and it was holding her back in growing her business because she felt she didn't have a voice. She thought she had worked through this trauma, but the work we do inside the program reopened the wound. I am not a professional therapist, I only coach from a place of my life circumstances, what I have encountered from being a student of life, and the tools I gained as a certified life coach. It wasn't the fact that she shared the information, what surprised me was the sheer volume of women on the Zoom that said #metoo. Some spoke up, some shared in the chat, some sent me a direct message after the call, and some just breathed it in. I don't know what weighed on my mind more: the number of women who had this experience in their childhood, or being a mother and wanting to overly protect my two daughters from this horrific trauma. Some of the women were in their fifties and sixties and that is the first time they publicly shared what they went through. I can't imagine the personal suffering of holding onto something for so many years or trying your hardest to act like it never happened.

Later that evening, I shared with Nick about the effect this coaching session had on me and he asked, "Did you share *your* story?"

My response was genuine, "What story?"

He said very directly as if shocked that I didn't remember. "Your abusive relationship in high school?"

I sat in complete shock. I realized I had buried the memory of that experience so far in my mind that I didn't remember until he said it. During the coaching session, I was so focused on the students that I didn't even think about myself. My experience wasn't sexual abuse, but abuse is abuse, no matter what form it comes in.

The last time I spoke of and maybe even thought about it, was when I shared it for the first time with Nick when we got serious in our relationship. Early into our dating, which didn't last long because we were engaged two-and-a-half months after we met, I struggled heavily with insecurity and jealousy. I had a giant wall around my heart that for anyone other than Nick was impenetrable.

When Nick would go out with friends after work, I was an intolerable ball of insecurity. The stories in my head had me convinced that he was cheating on me to the point it would make me physically sick. I had zero trust in him or any human with a Y chromosome. In my mind I was protecting myself by not fully giving my heart to someone, but I was in love, and these feelings were conflicting. I knew deep down that this wasn't a recipe for a good marriage and I needed to change, but I didn't know how. I had past relationship trauma that I brought into my relationship with Nick. Nick did nothing wrong, but I punished him for what another man had done to me twelve years earlier. This other man was my teenage boyfriend.

The summer going into my senior year of high school, I started dating a guy who was three years older than me who had a steady job. He was athletic and charming with demons that lay below his attractive smile. We had a lot of fun together and were quickly inseparable. We loved listening to country music, fishing, driving his truck in the mud, and drinking. He would cook me candlelight dinners, tell me how much he loved me, and how he never wanted to be without me.

I was in high school, so my days consisted of school, followed by basketball practice, coming home and eating dinner, then going to his house to hang out. All of my spare time, he wanted me to be with him and not with my friends, so that's what I did. When I did want to see my friends or go to a party, he would get angry; very angry. He would scream obscene names at me, tell me I was a slut, say my friends don't like me, and no other guy would ever stand being with me. My confidence and self-esteem were very low, so the only way I would respond was by crying. Then he would stop, hug me, and tell me he was sorry, and that he loved me. This vicious cycle would happen often. Screaming the worst insults you can to someone, followed by an apology, and a "You still love me right?"

Scared eighteen-year-old me would say, "Yes, of course." After a while, I wanted to avoid the fights, so I stopped going to anything that wasn't school- or sports-related.

One Saturday afternoon, we were at my house watching *The Goonies*. (Side note: I'm a product of the 1980s and this is hands down my favorite childhood movie.) An argument escalated as he was seated in a chair across the room from me. He started screaming with a vein bulging from his forehead, and he lunged toward me.

I tried to run but wasn't quick enough. He gripped both of my arms with his strong hands so we were face to face, then he picked me up so my feet were off the ground, threw me onto the couch, and jumped on top of me still yelling.

As I lay there crying and bruised, he told me it was my fault that he acted this way and if I wanted him to change, I needed to stop making him mad. I can still picture myself looking in the mirror and seeing bruises in the shape of handprints on my arms. Every night, I cried myself to sleep thinking if I wasn't good enough for this monster then who would want me. I was completely brainwashed.

His mom kicked him out of her house so I asked my parents if he could move in with us, and we instantly found ourselves in an episode of *Rosanne* with the boyfriend living in the basement, except it wasn't the basement, he was in the bedroom next to mine. Why I had done this when I was so miserable, I will never know. I was scared, insecure, and alone even when surrounded by people.

As a parent, I look back and wonder, *"What were my parents thinking to let that happen?"* But they are nice people and wanted to make me happy, so he lived with us for maybe three-to-six months. I was a shell of a person because I hid that I was in an emotionally and physically abusive relationship. Once he moved in, I lost a lot of weight. Eating felt like the only thing I could control, and if I looked like the skinny and pretty girls on TV, maybe he wouldn't be mean to me. I was weak and tired all the time because I was pushing my body to the limit, but to me it was the only way of dealing with the abuse.

When I finally mustered up the courage to end it and asked him to leave our house, I knew he would not take it well. When I heard his truck coming down the road, I told my mom to go into the basement because I was going to get rid of him and I didn't want her to witness whatever was about to happen. She obeyed. I met him in my pink bedroom, took a deep breath, and told him to get out of our house and that I no longer wanted to be with him. I remember speaking with a fake cockiness and attitude because that was the only leg I had to stand on.

He laughed at me and continued what he was doing. He said, "I told you no one else will ever love you, you are no good."

God stood by me while I said again in a stronger tone, "Get out!"

This time he aggressively turned around and grabbed both of my arms so we were face to face and he screamed at me, "NO ONE ELSE WILL WANT YOU!" Then he grabbed a gun that was in the corner of the room.

Now this may sound strange, but where I grew up this is common. Most men were hunters, and having a shotgun in the corner of the room was considered "protection." He had shotgun shells on the dresser, he wrote my name on a red one and put it in the barrel of the gun. I remember not wanting to run, because my mom was downstairs, and I didn't want him to do anything to her. I can still remember the sound of the chamber shutting, and him waiving the gun around carelessly with tears in his eyes saying he was going to kill himself.

In that moment, I realized how far this had gone. Small little words of brainwashing months ago led to that moment of life and death. As I witnessed this surreal moment, I wondered if he was really crazy enough to turn the gun on himself or me. He turned the gun towards me and I heard the words, "If I can't have you no one will."

It's said that before you die your life flashes before your eyes, and in that moment I saw myself as a little kid running and laughing in the yard, playing basketball with my mom in the driveway, and swimming at my aunt's house. I thought about my mom downstairs and what she was about to hear, and I thought how ironic that I was going to die in the pink room I grew up in as a sweet innocent girl. It was the longest moment of my life. I don't remember what happened next. I feel like I may have blacked out because he left the house.

My mom found me hysterically crying on the bedroom floor, and instead of holding me in safety, she walked into my room, grabbed a duffle bag, packed it, and said, "Go get in the car."

We didn't say much, and I didn't know where we were going until we pulled into my cousin's driveway. She told me to stay there until her and my dad got rid of him. They handled it and I didn't see him or hear from him again for a few weeks.

Because he had lived with us, he knew our family schedule. One day, he called our land line and I was the only one home, so I answered the phone. He was on his cell phone, pulling into the driveway, and he wanted to go for a drive so we could talk. I felt scared but confident that I could handle myself with him, so I got into his truck. Even as I type this, I can feel the same knot in my stomach as I did that day when we pulled out of the driveway and I knew I had made a mistake.

We drove around the back-country roads in silence. On these back roads, you can go for a while and not see another car. He sped through stop signs and I thought, "Oh my God, he is going to kill me, or both of us." I asked him to stop the car because I wanted to get out, and this only infuriated him.

He continued speeding and now swerved the truck all over the road. I told him I was going to jump out of the truck, and he sped up even more and told me to do it.

But when I went for the door handle, he slammed on the brakes and used his right hand to punch my left leg, then he pulled my hair so that my head was on the open seat between us and he began slapping and punching me.

I tried to fight back, but in my position I was defenseless and didn't know how to get him to stop. The next thing I knew, he grabbed my head from the seat and threw it against the passenger window which stunned me. He put the truck in drive, changed the radio station, and drove off like nothing happened. He drove to my parents' house, stopped the truck in front of the driveway, and I got out.

My final words to him were, "Never come near me again or I will call the police." That was the last day I feared for my life, but the lingering effects have always haunted me.

Typing this is extremely hard and makes me understand the women on my Zoom that afternoon. Our trauma may have been different, but the dark shadows it casts are the same. We spend so much of our life trying to forget the past that we end up living in it. Trying to resist the feelings that come along with the pain but failing to realize that feeling the pain is how we heal, grow, and learn from the experience.

It wasn't until the #metoo coaching session and reliving my own abusive relationship, that I finally understood the true meaning of *things don't happen to you they happen for you*. I would secretly ask, "Why would God want bad circumstances to happen *for* you?" It's the word *for* that created the confusion, but the fog of confusion was lifted that day and clarity was reached. Without realizing it, I created a safe space for women to share their deepest secrets to expose a part of them they had kept hidden for many years.

- I had mine hidden too.
- I can relate.
- I was hurt too.
- I am a victim too.
- I understand.
- I feel you.
- I hear you.
- I am you.

We have spent our entire lives trying to forget the circumstance that brought us pain. We push through the hard things, shove them deep down, and turn to alcohol, drugs, or other vices to help us forget. However, learning to fully feel your feelings has been one of the hardest yet most liberating experiences of my life. There is a box of Kleenex permanently on my desk because ugly cries happen, and I don't fight them. When it happens, I say "thank you" and release it, because I know it is pain leaving my body and I am healing.

If you are struggling with past trauma, please stop hiding from it and trying to forget what happened. You can never live the authentic life you desire if there is a piece of you locked away. By holding on to anger, the only person that is suffering is you. It's not your fault, you are worthy of more and you deserve better. I'm not saying that you need to forgive that person for the horrible thing they did. Every circumstance in our life has the potential to increase or stunt our growth. Don't allow that evil person to stunt your growth. They have done for long enough already and it's time you take your power back. Have the willingness to release the hold the past has on you.

I get asked a lot, "How do I let it go?"

My answer is always the same: choose to change the story attached to the circumstance. The only place the past lives is in your thoughts. Everything that happens in life we assign a meaning to. For your traumatic experience you may have made it mean you are wrong, you are bad, you are not enough or worthy and that is the story you keep telling yourself. Each moment we have a choice to change the meaning. You are the author of your life, not the reader. You hold the pen to change the narrative. Here is a way to rewrite your story: *No longer will you have power over my life. I did nothing wrong. I am a strong person who deserves happiness, health, love, and prosperity in my life. I will use my story to create awareness and inspire others to heal their traumas, because no one can take my spirit away.*

Never internalize being done wrong to as being wrong. Other people's inexcusable behavior is an indictment on their character, not yours.

The Dogpile

You Gotta Believe!

— Tug McGraw

IN BASEBALL, THE WORD "DOGPILE" IS ASSOCIATED WITH victory. The dogpile typically begins where the last out of the game is made in a really big game like the conference championship or the World Series. In 2015, Nick started the baseball program at Cabrini University in the suburbs of Philadelphia. At his very first practice, he had the team do a dogpile and vision cast the end result they were working toward. As a new program, their end goal was to win the conference championship and dogpile on their home field in front of their fans. The dogpile signifies success, hard work paying off; the ultimate end result. It's a feeling and moment every player and coach desires.

The inaugural season for the Cabrini Cavaliers in 2017 did not result in a dogpile. With a team of mainly freshmen, there were more ass-kickings received then given that year. With a season beginning in

February on the east coast, we quickly learned the meaning behind, "It's always colder when you are losing."

The 2018 season had the same vision of meeting at the dogpile. The season was very exciting, and they made it to the conference tournament but came in fourth place. The dogpile was in sight but didn't happen for the Cavaliers that year.

The 2019 season was the most fun I have ever had as a spectator. The team went 31-11, was the number one seed in the conference, hosted the conference tournament at their field, and lost the championship game. They watched another team dogpile on their field. That's a tougher gut punch than losing the actual game.

The 2020 season began in February and this team and the coaches were ready. They knew without a doubt this was their year to make the dogpile happen on their field and finally have the first practice vision brought to life. Thirteen games into the season and COVID put a stop to the world and baseball. No dogpile.

When college resumed in person in January 2021, baseball was back with a limited schedule, but at least they were allowed to play again. The freshmen from the first ass whooping season were now seniors and had a chip on their shoulders. The victory and dogpile was a laser focus and the only thing that mattered. They had unfinished business, and it was now their time to bring home the first conference championship in program history. The regular conference season ended with Nick and his squad in second place, so the championship games were to be held at the first seed home field in Washington D.C. It didn't matter to the Cavs, they were prepared to walk onto another team's field, play with heart, and have their dogpile moment.

It's not often that you get to see your spouse at work. When Nick coaches, I witness his passion. I love watching him coach. I watch him construct a mental chess match with his players and always try to stay two-to-three moves ahead of the other coach. It took me a while to understand the brilliance and strategy of the game. It's a very smart game, and I respect why he loves it so much.

On a sunny Friday morning in May, I had our girls play hooky from school, and the three of us piled into my SUV for the three-hour drive to watch Daddy and his team win the championship. My heart burst with pride and I was so excited to watch these boys that now have become men in the four years they waited for their moment. Two hours into our drive, I received a phone call from one of the player's moms and when I answered with an excited, "Hello!"

She firmly said, "Did Nick call you and tell you what happened?"

I give Nick space on game day and during the season for that matter. If there is something I need to know he will tell me, if not I don't ask. I told her I hadn't talked to Nick and was about an hour from the field. My heart sank as I asked her, "What happened?" I knew from the tone of her voice that her response wasn't going to be positive.

She began to tell me that nine players from our team were being sent back to Philadelphia.

" What!?" The best player and center fielder received an email while enroute to D.C. that contained one word that forever left an imprint on people's lives that day. That one word—positive—had a ripple effect that I don't think anyone could have predicted. One player received a positive COVID test and, due to contact tracing, nine players, mostly the starters for the game, had to leave the field immediately. No questions asked.

The only thing I could do was cry. I was so sad. My heart broke for the boys who were ending their baseball career with this memory. Literally on the doorstep of the biggest game of their career and because of one word the opportunity was stripped from them. I was sad for Nick and the other coaches who work countless hours and sacrifice family time and personal time to give the team the best shot at winning.

But the game still had to go on. Nick had to reconfigure his whole game plan and line up. The players that took the field that day played with all their hearts and left everything they had on the diamond for two games. I cheered louder than I ever had that day with a secret hope that my cheer would help fix the day and put points on the board. After two games and six hours of baseball, the season came to an end. There was no dogpile, only tears and long embraces.

I didn't talk to Nick in between the games and, honestly, I wasn't ready to. In these situations, I feel like I am supposed to be the rock, the steady one, but all I kept thinking was, *I don't know how to wife this. I don't know what I am supposed to say or do to fix it.* My natural tendency is to fix things or make things happen. That's my strong suit. I move into action. But this time, I was helpless. I couldn't fix it, and I didn't know how to process the feelings or be strong for him. When I finally saw Nick in the hotel room that night, all we did was hold each other and cry. I said to him, "I'm so sorry."

All he kept saying was, "Don't be sorry for me. Be sorry for these boys and an opportunity stolen from them."

Two years in a row, COVID took away the championship. Losing is one thing, but not having the opportunity to know the true outcome hurts differently. The next day felt like a funeral. There was a dark cloud over everyone's heads. No one spoke much. Everyone just wanted to leave D.C. and get back to Philadelphia. The sadness in our home Saturday night was palpable. Nick's heart was broken, and I couldn't fix it. I could only watch and hug. I didn't know how to look for the silver lining in this one.

Early the next morning, Nick gathered himself and headed to the university for graduation day. He smiled through the pain and celebrated the young men for their four-year accomplishment. Their opportunity was shattered the day before, and now they had to look forward to a new opportunity of life in the real world. It's not the ending anyone wanted, but it was the one that had to be accepted.

I don't know if I have ever been more grateful for Sunday morning and 9 a.m. mass as I was on this day. The girls and I got to church, and I went on my knees and started talking to the Big Guy.

"God, I trust and I have faith, but I just don't know what you are doing here. You need to give me a little direction on why this happened." I'm a woman of faith and I pray a lot. Some days my prayers are answered, and some days I need to learn the lesson and that is the answer. This particular day, I was very direct: I needed clarity. Then I had a moment. A moment that I will never forget. With my eyes shut, and my hands clenched together while on my knees, I heard His voice loud and clear.

The voice said, "They are meant to dogpile on their field."

I instantly began to cry happy tears of relief. I felt a weight lifted off my shoulders at that moment. I now understand why it happened. If they had played with their full roster that day they would have won, they would have had the dogpile, but not on their home field. They are meant to dogpile on their field, in front of their fans, and have the moment they created at their first practice.

When I saw Nick at home later that day I said, "I know why it happened." He gave me a perplexed look and was eager to listen. I told him that God spoke to me today and gave me the answer, "The team wasn't meant to dogpile in D.C. You are meant to dogpile on your own field."

I watched the color come back to his face and took a deep sigh. He grabbed his phone and I assume texted his best friend in baseball, his assistant coach, Rod. It didn't take away the pain of what happened, but the shift in perspective sparked a flame that relit a fire that had smoldered the day before.

This is one of the best lessons I have ever learned. The circumstance stayed the same: they lost the game, but our thoughts around it changed. Our thoughts shifted from, *Why did this happen?* to *We are determined to dogpile on our field.* This lesson reinforced in me the power of choice. We have complete control of how we view each circumstance that happens in our life. We can choose to see it as an obstacle or an opportunity, because we choose the meaning. Our thoughts hold all the power. The question is how many of us actually use this power to create the results we desire in our lives?

You've Always Had the Power

> If you don't get lost, there's a chance you will never be found.
>
> — Anonymous

THE SIMPLE ACT OF WAKING UP ONE HOUR EARLIER, AVOIDING social media and email during that time, and creating a safe space for myself to pay attention to my thoughts is what recalibrated my life. I can directly connect the awareness of my thoughts and quality of my life today to my Selfish Hour. I gave a gift to myself that, although very difficult at times, eventually helped me reclaim my power. I learned not only who I was and who I am, but more importantly, who I want to be everyday to be an example to others.

I wake up each morning with a purpose, and that feeling alone is priceless. Myka is still with me, she tries often to protect me each time I want to up level my life or step outside my comfort zone. I clearly understand her role and acknowledge her, I tell her we are safe then ask her to leave. The doubt, fear, and "I am stupid" thoughts sadly don't go away. I have just created an awareness of their presence and use the tools I just shared with you to redirect myself back to confident action. And if don't move back to confident action, I know I am choosing to stay in my story.

I choose who I want to be each day. Some moments I choose gratitude, some moments I choose bitterness and self-pity. It doesn't matter to me that I feel self-pity sometimes, because I know I am choosing it. I went through a phase of trying to only see the positive in everything, wearing clothing with positive quotes and viewing the world with a glass half full mentality. However, it's not meant to be that way. We can't understand joy, happiness, and fulfillment if we haven't experienced sadness, disappointment, and regret. You can't fully appreciate one without the other. They are both important to the experience of life.

I have taught myself to feel my feelings from beginning to end without trying to interrupt or alter them. This simple yet profound process is what has given me the power to choose. I can also choose my way out of it and back to gratitude. Some days I choose to be sassy, but I know I am in complete control and it's my decision. I am not reacting; I am consciously choosing how I want to respond. Even if my response is a negative one. I choose it and I can choose something different when I feel ready. I will often set a timer when I feel a negative emotion toward someone or something and allow myself to sit in that feeling for five to ten minutes, then, when the timer goes off, I do my best to release it and move my thoughts back to gratitude.

We are surrounded with countless choices every single day. What to wear, what to eat, what music to listen to, how to respond to a situation, what to click on social media, or what new show to binge on. Everything is a choice. Unconsciously, we have created so many habits that don't feel like choices anymore it's just what we do or who we are.

Even personality tests tell you who you are, so you continue to show up as that person or say "I'm an Enneagram 8; that's why I act like this." I'm not saying these aren't accurate, but what if you want to think or act differently tomorrow? I take a personality test every couple of years and they are always different because I am constantly evolving. I grow more open each year, and the cynicism that I once thought of as "how I was raised" is no longer there. The more I read, travel, and meet amazing people from all different backgrounds, the more my world expands, which causes my thoughts to become deeper. This has also shown me how little I truly know and the thirst keeps me always wanting to introduce myself to new experiences.

When I look back over the past couple of years, I can see that the biggest transformation I made is from moving my thoughts from fear to love. I used to show up and view my life from a place of fear:

- Fear of what others thought.
- Fear of not hitting my goals.
- Fear of the pandemic.
- Fear of my internal thoughts.
- Fear of my feelings.
- Fear of the unknown.
- Fear of my family never reconnecting.
- Fear of never giving myself to my true potential.
- Fear of not being a good example to my daughters.

I operated from a place of fear, worry, and scarcity because it felt normal and comfortable. I was consumed by it without knowing it. I knew love and I felt love, but my core thoughts were rooted in fear. This process taught me how to shift myself to love and trust. Surrendering the need to be right, releasing expectations of who people are supposed to be, and embracing silence to hear my own thoughts has changed my entire life. I learned how to put love at the center of everything.

It started with learning to love myself without judgement which allowed me to love Myka and embrace my flaws and shortcomings without reasoning. Sometimes I wake up in the middle of the night and begin to worry. When this feeling overwhelms me I instantly tell myself "I am good, life is good" and I repeat it until I feel my energy shift. When you can change your thoughts, it changes your feelings, which in turn changes your actions, and ultimately your results. If you want different results in life, all you need to do is change your thoughts and it sends a ripple effect to the results. The hard part is staying consistent in shifting your thoughts and repeating them until you truly see the results change. It's simple, not easy, but very simple. Creating the consistency builds trust with yourself, so you know your changed thoughts, change your life.

These techniques are not new. This is just the way I interpreted and implemented them into my life to create real change. You can too. It's the daily practices added into your routines that will help guide your journey. From someone who changed her life by changing her thoughts, I strongly encourage you to take what you learned here and make small adjustments in your life. You deserve it, you are worth it, and you can do it!

In 1939, Glinda the Good Witch from *The Wizard of Oz* eloquently summed up my book in one sentence when she said, "You've always had the power my dear, you just had to learn it for yourself."

Resources

NATIONAL DOMESTIC VIOLENCE HOTLINE: 24 HOURS A DAY, 7 days a week: 1- 800-799-7233

NATIONAL SEXUAL ASSAULT HOTLINE: 24 HOURS A DAY, 7 DAYS a week: 1-800-656-4673

ALCOHOLICS ANONYMOUS HTTPS://WWW.AA.ORG/

Acknowledgments

To be at the acknowledgement section of the book is a bold reminder that I actually completed it. Writing this book has not been an easy or quick journey but it's been a memorable one that healed and liberated me. I am forever a changed woman because of the journey I took myself on and then reliving it a second time with writing this book.

I firmly believe that people enter our lives for a season, a reason or a lifetime. Regardless of their length in our lives, each have some sort of purpose. Whether we choose to receive and learn from the purpose is up to us.

Here are some of people that have come into my life and I received their purpose.

First and foremost, I would like to thank all the wonderful people that have allowed me to coach them and the people who are yet to come. Being able to share my knowledge to help others is the greatest gift I can ever give. I will always create a safe space for you to be vulnerable and grow. I am grateful for all of you.

I want to thank those who helped birth this book. My editor and publisher Deborah Kevin, from the moment we first connected via Zoom, I knew you were the right person to bring my words to life. Thank you for having patience with me to learn and understand the process to evolve from writer to author. Heike Martin, thank you for your amazing photography skills and pushing your creative limits with me. Hanne Brøter, thank you for capturing the essence of the book with only a picture. Suzanne T. Moore, thank you for being an amazing launch partner and teaching me all the ways to get my book into the hands of the people who need it. My book cohort who held space for me to share my fears and emotions with the launch: you are a talented group of women that I was honored to go on this journey with.

Sometimes people come into your life for a season then leave and re-enter for a lifetime. Bob, you are that person for me. I am forever grateful for you because you taught me how to dream and we joined forces to make dreams become reality. Thank you for your friendship, mentorship, and bringing me on as your first coach. We always said we were going to do big things together and here we are...just getting started.

Nicole Lewis-Keeber and Jessica Barnak, thank you for being strong women in my corner when I was becoming a Corporate Refugee. Nicole, thank you for the talk in Denver before my presentation. It forever changed me.

To Lisa, thank you for the memorable talks over the years and helping redirect my thoughts on many occasions. I picked the right confirmation sponsor because you are still doing your part to be a positive impact in my life.

I want to acknowledge my very best lifetime friend, Ashley aka Pea. I am forever grateful for our friendship, the countless hours we have talked about everything and nothing, for 11K, and for the honesty and respect we have for each other. You are the most beautiful person inside and out and my life is better with you in it.

To my Aunt Helen, the woman I have admired the longest in my life. You paved the path for me to move out of Ohio when you took me to Paris and opened my eyes to a whole new world. I wouldn't be where I am today if it weren't for your love and support. Thank you for always believing in me.

Taylor, thanks for coming full circle in my life. I love working on our relationship and getting to know each other now. You are a beautiful and intelligent person who I am proud to call my niece.

To my family. Mom, you have always been my biggest cheerleader and #1 fan. I appreciate all the sacrifices you made to get me to where I am today. Thanks for your support, love, and kind heart. Dad, I understand you more than you realize. To my brothers, you both have taught me lessons and helped me grow and for that I am eternally grateful.

I especially want to acknowledge my beautiful daughters, Codi and Devney. I know one day you will read this book and learn about a different side of your mom. Part of me had a lot of fear knowing that but the bigger part of me knows that I am doing my best to be a great example for you two—to show you that no matter what challenge you face in life, you can get through it and become stronger because of it. It's an honor to be your mom, the greatest joy I have in life is watching you grow up. Love love.

Lastly to Nick, thank you for winking at me, thank you for asking me the pivotal question that sparked this whole journey, and thank you for always giving me the loving push to be my best. Your drive and determination to follow your dreams allow me to follow mine. Thank you for the way you love me, support me, and give me space when I need it. This book and my life wouldn't be possible without you. I love you Nick—let's keep chasing dreams.

About the Author

Photo credit: Heike Martin

After thirteen seemingly successful years climbing the corporate ladder, Megan Weisheipl realized her ladder was leaning on the wrong building. She took a risk, becoming a corporate refugee and launching a coaching business. She became a Certified Life Coach and the Director of Coaching for *Your Virtual Upline.* Megan helps women transform their lives by simply transforming their thoughts. Through coaching and speaking she guides women to step into their greatness. Megan focuses on releasing the self-imposed obligation to people-please and overcoming imposter syndrome by creating confidence in being the authentic YOU.

Megan lives in East Norriton, PA, with her husband Nick and their two spunky daughters Codi and Devney. She loves a good cup of coffee, laughing until it hurts, *Friends* re-runs and beginning her day on the Peloton. You can connect with her at www.meganspeaks.com.

facebook.com/megan.phillipsweisheipl

instagram.com/meganweisheipl

About the Publisher

Highlander Press, founded in 2019, is a mid-sized publishing company committed to diversity and sharing big ideas thereby changing the world through words.

Highlander Press guides authors from where they are in the writing-editing-publishing process to where they have an impactful book of which they are proud, making a long-time dream come true. Having authored a book improves your confidence, helps create clarity, and ensures that you claim your expertise.

What makes Highlander Press unique is that their business model focuses on building strong collaborative relationships with other women-owned businesses, which specialize in some aspect of the publishing industry, such as graphic design, book marketing, book launching, copyrights, and publicity. The mantra "a rising tide lifts all boats" is one they embrace.

linkedin.com/in/highlanderpress

facebook.com/highlanderpress

instagram.com/highlanderpress

Made in the USA
Coppell, TX
02 May 2023